MAN AT PLAY

MAN AT PLAY

Nine Centuries of Pleasure Making

JOHN ARMITAGE

FREDERICK WARNE

Published by
FREDERICK WARNE & CO LTD: LONDON
FREDERICK WARNE & CO INC: NEW YORK
1977

© *Frederick Warne & Co Ltd 1977*

To Margaret, my wife,
who once bowled
a Bishop out
for 0

ISBN 0 7232 2018 2

Filmset and printed in Great Britain by
BAS Printers Limited, Wallop, Hampshire

☆ CONTENTS ☆

☆ LIST OF ILLUSTRATIONS ☆

6

Man at Play

☆ *PREFACE* ☆

It will be plain to readers, I am sure, that I have been greatly indebted to a host of historians, poets, diarists, travellers, letter writers and others whose work, though only briefly concerned with my subject, has brought hours of renewed pleasure. Under the circumstances it seemed impossible to compile a short bibliography and a long one seemed inappropriate to my slender narrative. So I express my gratitude to them here, dead though so many of them are, and admit that the only trouble they gave me was in the selection of possible quotations. There were hundreds equally apposite and amusing to the ones I have used.

I also take this opportunity for saying my thanks to Veronica Bridges and the other librarians of Letchworth Public Library for the enthusiastic and willing assistance they give to all their customers including myself at all times. Although I was once told, some years ago, that I must be costing the ratepayers a lot of money, the spirit of the remark was that librarians wish that more not fewer people would take advantage of the excellent services the Public Library system can provide. My thanks also to Ann Chambers, another librarian, and her husband Tony for taking so much care in looking up references for me, and to Michael Kelly, Chief Executive, North Herts District Council, for loaning me heavy volumes and finding me a place to consult them.

Finally I was fortunate in being able to have Barbara Hilborne, a former colleague of mine, to look after the illustrations, excellent sub-editors to improve the text, and Geoffrey Payton to take care of the index.

. . . genuine, pure play is one of the main bases of civilization.

Johan Huizinga. *Homo Ludens*

For such is our nature, that we cannot stand long bent, but we must have our relaxations as well of mind, as of body.

H. Peacham. *English Recreations in 1641*

Therefore we cannot understand . . . unless we are willing to bear constantly in mind two complementary truths: first, the essential similarity of human nature in all ages: and, secondly, the dissimilarity of men's environment . . .

G. G. Coulton. *Medieval Panorama*

It were a curious study to trace the progress of public taste in matters of amusement, and to endeavour to investigate the causes of the variety of changes it has undergone.

Knight's *London*

☆ *BEFORE THE OFF* ☆

Samuel Johnson defined play in his dictionary as 'to do something not as a task, but for a pleasure'. It is not a complete description but it is a useful one for it goes to the heart of the matter. Playing is for pleasure or, better perhaps, for fun. Such a definition makes it clear that the schoolboy of an earlier generation, compelled against his wishes to participate at cricket, was not playing. Only when the compulsion was negligible, because the action coincided so exactly with his own choice, could he be said to be playing.

Likewise the actress is not playing when she appears on the stage; nor is the professional footballer on Saturday afternoons. Both are working. The footballer looks as if he is playing and his admirers may think that he is, but he is not on the field by choice but of necessity and his play is not for fun. On the other hand the audience at the theatre and the men and women watching the football match *are* playing. And judging by their laughter, shouts and groans they are playing fairly hard. They have come to the theatre or the football ground by choice and they can go away again whenever they choose.

There is a further and, at first sight, curious point about play. It is only real or true play if it is played to known and accepted rules. Without rules a player cannot have fun for, if the actions of his fellows are wholly unpredictable—including perhaps walking away with the ball—play is frustrating. Even if a man is playing by himself almost the first thing that he does is to decide on the rules; he needs a framework of certainty to make the action enjoyable. Listen to children playing and the most likely wail at some moment is: 'That's not fair!' 'Who says?', may be the menacing retort, but if possible this is ignored because all the players know what the accepted rules are.

Play is as natural to animals as it is to man. An example of instinctive understanding of play and the acceptance of rules is that of a dog playing with a boy and a ball. The rules have not been explained to the dog or the boy but both know what is play and what is not. Generally the dog will 'play fair' so long as the boy does or until he gets bored—the same rule that he follows when playing with another dog. Thus, if cornered, he will, after growling ferociously (which is part of the play), give the ball up, promptly wagging his tail for the game to begin again. If, however, the boy, tiring perhaps of his lack of success, gets rough or calls up too strong reinforcements, the dog lies down or walks away because he recognizes that play is over when the action is no longer fun. Adults, before the codification of rules and the appointment of referees in the nineteenth century, had similar problems. Fights often

11

broke out because the rules were either too few for enjoyment or disregarded, but generally the accepted rules, like those of children's games, were locally well understood, and remained sufficient until matches began to be arranged with teams from some distance away.

This book also deals with the many different ways in which a man expects to get satisfaction from his play, and the changes that influence his choice of play at different times. No attempt is made to discuss the subject of day-dreams, which in a psychological sense are a major part of his play. The book is concentrated on man's external play and how this changes according to circumstances while still meeting the same fundamental needs. It will be clear enough why a quotation from Professor Coulton's *Medieval Panorama* is put with others at the beginning of this book: there is an 'essential similarity of human nature in all ages'.

Most men are competitive and this is reflected in their play. The degree of competitiveness varies considerably but it is nearly always there even when the player has no opponent but himself. There are occasions when he rests from competitiveness, goes fishing alone, swims lazily in the sea or is bird-watching. Resting in this way is still playing.

The kind of play a man chooses depends upon his nature, his environment, his mood and his age, for most men must satisfy more than one need through play. Young men, particularly, have need to rid themselves of surplus energy and feelings of aggression and find their satisfaction in a Rugby scrum or in some other physical contact game. Older men and some women may get this satisfaction vicariously by watching young men assaulting one another on the football field or in individual combat in a ring.

Other young men, with plenty of physical energy but less aggression may choose quieter games or sports, perhaps cross-country running or swimming. Many have need to display their skill in physical control: to themselves as well as to others. Gymnasts on the bar and divers on the high board may be pleased with the thought, and stimulated by it, that others are watching, but at the moment of execution it is likely that the keenest pleasure comes from the achievement of the performance, even if that is greater in the mind than in fact. The same applies to the stroke at cricket or the well-laid pass at football. Applause is sweet music but it means less if the play was 'right'.

Team games offer major satisfactions beyond the competitiveness of the match. There is pleasure in acting in unison with others, of weaving a purposeful pattern leading to a goal or a try; the communal bath and the visit to the pub are part of the ritual, which if removed would lack ingredients that have long since been regarded as essential to the play. Something of the same pleasure is enjoyed by the spectators. Watching a match on television at home stirs the mind to create satisfactory images but it lacks the excitement of the walk to the match with the expectant crowd, the felt emotion filling the ground and the catharsis that follows, making tea and home a further prospect of pleasure. It is the same with spectacles, the manufactured play that promotes wonder, amusement, even fear, provided that the experience is shared. Spectacles have been used for quieting the people in ancient and modern times, in Rome and in Spain. Rome made the mistake of feeding a love

of violence by offering bigger and bigger spectacles of bestial horror. Modern Spain might be said to have gauged correctly the needs of individuals and society by providing entertainment which has as its climax the ritual killing of the bull, the bull being both victim and idol. Because the majority is not in need of such spectacles it does not necessarily follow that they have no value to the community. Some believe that outlets for passionate feelings have been badly neglected in most Western countries and that some compensation for the law and order of urban living should be made available.

There is another interesting aspect of man's play when he is watching others. This is his need to associate with a team or player on the field of play. In theory he can watch the play of others dispassionately, not needing to seek success for one or another of the contestants. In practice he cannot do this. He must associate; otherwise the fun fails.

Man uses play for other purposes than aggression, physical exertion, tranquillity and demonstrations of skill to evoke admiration or for his own self-satisfaction. One of these is social. In every century men and women were brought together socially through dance and music, but it was only in the nineteenth century that women, hard pressed to find means of escaping from an unnatural confinement to the drawing room, discovered games (including bicycling) and were allowed to play.

It is not easy to determine why running after something should have a universal appeal, but it does. Children have invented games to include the chase; old men and women stop in their tracks to watch a man pursuing nothing more animated than his hat. Even the gentle poet, William Cowper, first made a reputation with his poem on John Gilpin and wrote an amusingly descriptive letter on the pursuit of a tame hare. Many disapprove of fox hunting but find it hard to resist the thrill of dogs, horses and men streaming across the field in pursuit of a small animal. In medieval times it is possible that part of the pleasure of the rough games of football was regarding the ball as a quarry to be chased; a poor man's substitute for the real thing.

It is only in the twentieth century that the poorer and the rich have begun to live even approximately the same kind of lives. The redistribution of wealth has brought about a revolution in activities and all but the very poor have been able to mimic the play patterns of the privileged. In 1801, when Joseph Strutt wrote his famous book *The Sports and Pastimes of the People of England*, such a situation was hardly conceivable. In consequence Strutt organized his book into four sections: I. Rural Exercises Practised by Persons of Rank; II. Rural Exercises Generally Practised; III. Pastimes Usually Exercised in Towns and Cities, or Places Adjoining to Them; IV. Domestic Amusements of Various Kinds and Pastimes Appropriated to Particular Seasons. Much will be said in this book about the division of play between rich and poor. Fundamentally, and before the results of the industrial revolution had had time to take effect, the division was a question of land. If a man held land he played; if he held a great deal of land he played even harder. It was his inalienable right, not to be questioned, not to be doubted. Yet all through the 900 years covered here some did doubt and some did

A day out with the Oxford drag, early nineteenth century

On the river, a late Victorian and Edwardian pleasure

Village cricket in the twentieth century

question. Some did even more: they poached. Their punishment, if caught, was severe but poaching could not be put down. The extra and better food was a great temptation, but so also was the play, a chance to pit one's wits and skill against the hired protectors of the not always unkindly establishment.

This book, then, is a report about how man has played throughout nine centuries and the environmental changes that have modified his play. It is also an attempt to show—the compulsion to play being so very strong—how each class of society has seized its opportunity to play, while denying the privilege to others for as long as possible if it interfered with their work. It is not suggested that the powerful in society were aware of what they were doing in refusing play to others. It did not occur to many of them that play was vital to the well-being of all or, as Professor Huizinga put it, that play was one of the main bases of civilization. They just thought that play was their due alone. Only the rich played for a substantial part of the day in most centuries but the effect of the industrial and social revolutions by 1975 had been to curtail the playtime of the rich and to increase that of all others. Whether in the process enough time had been left for work is a problem, happily outside the scope of this volume.

1

☆ *MEDIEVAL BACKCLOTH* ☆

Mainly twelfth and thirteenth centuries

The privilege that Joseph Strutt (*The Sports and Pastimes of the People of England*) associated with the holding of land was everywhere apparent in the years following the Conquest. Domesday Book had confirmed it. Land was the reward that men looked for in return for services and the holding of it conferred power, duties and indulgences. These indulgences within the framework of the feudal system, with the king at its apex, included opportunities for play that were of right, and refused to others. The poor had no rights and their chance of play came only on holy days when it was limited to such enjoyments as would not infringe a landowner's interests.

It seems strange, therefore, to read the words of Richard FitzNigel (justice-itinerant 1179; Bishop of London 1189) declaring that the forests were the secret places of kings where they went to hunt, put away their cares and have some peace. Yet, in fact, they were just that. Being a king at this period was to be in a constant state of progress around the country, hearing petitions, administering justice and making sure that no baron was growing too powerful. Wars kept the king abroad some of the time but at home there was no means of getting away from it all except in the Forest, which had been declared his personal property, and where he had built hunting lodges to accommodate himself and his retinue in preference to staying with bishops and barons whose ideas of hospitality were bound to include too much eating and drinking and too many grumbles and demands.

The areas known as the Forest were not continuous; nor were they entirely covered by trees. They were those parts of the country, mainly in the south and west (see map p. 18), where the beasts of the chase had taken refuge. The Normans were prodigiously fond of hunting. They did not acquire the taste for it in England but brought it with them, so it must have appeared a heaven-sent reward to William when he discovered how great the opportunity for hunting in England was to be. He immediately declared these forest areas to be his and put a stop to the gradual encroachments of the plough which, as local populations grew, had been the natural order of things before the Conquest. In his view he was not denying food to the poor so much as protecting the 'venison' (the deer and the boar) from extinction. At all costs the venison must be preserved for him.

It is practically impossible to exaggerate the importance of the Forest to Norman kings. At one time it was said to cover a third of the kingdom. It embraced whole villages and great areas of scrub-land. It had clauses devoted to it in Magna Carta (1215) and these were reviewed and re-stated in the Forest Charter of 1217. The poor who were unfortunate enough to live in

The probable extent of the king's forest

the designated areas were under a tyranny, and even the rich were restricted in the use of their own land if part of it was included. To the poor these conditions were not entirely new for something like the same situation had been known before the Conquest. There was, however, one mighty difference. The Normans not only had a passion for hunting; they brought with them a managerial revolution. Nothing like Norman thoroughness in maintaining forest law had been previously experienced, and gone now was the sporting chance for the poor man to add a cony to the pot without fear of cruel punishment. Even his dogs were in constant danger. They were likely to be shot at sight if found trespassing and in any case it was the duty of their owners to have them 'lawed' (that is three of the claws on the front paws removed). Perhaps it was not everywhere quite as bad as the court rolls suggest, as evidence about kindness, slackness and turning a blind eye is always wanting, but it was certainly bad enough.

The barons could not hunt the venison in the Forest unless in the presence of the king or by special dispensation for an unusual reason. However, if the Forest was part of their land or was contiguous with it they were usually permitted to hunt the lesser game: hares, foxes, badgers, otters, polecats, weasels and in one list at least, the lobster. This was called rights of warren. Similar permissions were granted to abbots and other dignitaries of the Church, who thus began a centuries' long link with the chase which, even at the start, was often a scandal. 'Chase' is a word that was also used in medieval times to describe an area of land which the king allowed a baron or an abbot to establish for keeping his own beasts of the chase. Historically this chase is

18

important, for the privilege conveyed soon led to the establishment of rich men's parks and thus, several centuries later, when the Forest Law had fallen into disuse, to a demand for their protection. It was obtained through the Game Laws, which, as far as the poor were concerned, were equally tyrannous.

There was one animal the poor could kill in the Forest if they happened, which was unlikely, to meet it. That was the wolf. The wolf was not hunted in England as it was in Germany; instead it was 'outlawed' which meant in practice that it could be killed on sight and a reward claimed. The wolf's status was so unique that a man who was outlawed was said to be marked with the sign of the wolf.

The villein, a man who cultivated some land on sufferance from his lord, and who lived in one of the villages or hamlets of the Forest was handicapped positively as well as negatively. In one respect he was in the position of an Exmoor farmer today who is pledged not to shoot deer in the interest of the hunt; instead he must do what he can to fence his crops, and if this fails must bear the consequences and await compensation: there was, however, no compensation for the villein and little chance of fencing. If he killed a deer he faced imprisonment and fines which he could not hope to pay. The Forest Law also protected the trees and the scrub in which the beasts of the chase made their lairs. There was some latitude over the gathering of fallen wood but even this was not a right. The army of forest wardens—hated men in most areas, like the game-keepers of the future—was supported by a system of special Forest courts. The courts were kept busy by the poachers and by hungry and frustrated villagers, while the records reveal that a few friendly or less dedicated foresters existed who were punished in their turn for showing lack of zeal. Zeal was sometimes extended to include 'scot ales', the brewing of ale by the forest wardens and the intimidating of villagers into buying it. As was to be expected the poacher had plenty of friends, even in court, and the warden few.

Although the few medieval pictures that exist show the king and his companions having a good gallop after their prey it must not be imagined that there was much resemblance to a fox hunt of the present day. The king, and others, hunted with a mixed pack: dogs to drive the beast from his lair, strong dogs to attack and kill, and swift dogs to pursue if the quarry got away. The king's party would wait in a clearing for the huntsmen to drive the animal out of the thickets, and would shoot when it broke cover. It was not an easy task to kill with an arrow shot from the mounted position and the probability was that the animal was first wounded and then finally despatched when the dogs had pulled it down. The pleasure of the day, for the king, was in the freedom he enjoyed when making his choice of how to spend his time, the absence of suitors of all kinds, the fresh air after too many committee hours, the possibility of danger, the shooting skill, the work of the dogs and the physical tiredness at the end of it. An ideal form of play for those who liked it, and undisturbed at that time by the moralizing of others.

The younger set among the knights preferred the tournaments, the mock battles not to be confused with the later gentlemanly combats between two heavily armed figures in the lists. The records bear witness to the king's anger and the Church's consternation at the disorderly behaviour caused by these tournaments, not unlike the wild sprees of the Regency bucks or the outbreaks of violence of football hooligans in modern times. The excuse for having tournaments was that they provided training for war, as army manoeuvres do now; but they were certainly not under discipline and in practice were a gigantic game. Moreover the play was highly competitive and rough. For big occasions sides were chosen to promote natural enmities: North *v* South and England *v* France. French knights came to England to play, and English knights went to France, the birthplace of the tournament. Rules were negligible. The battle was fought on horseback first, and then on foot if a knight was unhorsed. Feasting followed the battle. A few knights were killed in the fighting, and not all accidentally for feuds grew up between individuals who used the tournaments to further them. Some kings tried to control the situation by restricting the places where tournaments could be held to designated sites in open country close to suitable main roads. Fees were charged for those wishing to take part. Other kings tried to ban the tournaments altogether, but without much success; knights had little else to do but prepare for war, and were hopeful that through war they would get land. Tournaments did not die out until the middle of the fourteenth century. Meantime schools of swordmanship were growing up in all the Western capitals and these too were sources of trouble for the authorities.

It was much the same story at the universities, where students were forever in violent conflict with townspeople. Lacking organized outlets for their physical needs and having far too much time on their hands, students were free to do much as they liked which included the least damaging action of absenting themselves from their studies as often and for as long as they felt inclined. The biggest danger to the community was presumed to be on national saints' days and at Cambridge feasts were specifically forbidden on such days.

Ball play also disturbed the peace. Students were forbidden to play tennis and other ball games in the streets but it is clear that they often did so. Buckler play was condemned; so was the more plebeian sport of combat with staffs. Altogether the townspeople had a hard if not impossible job to make their streets safe, all the more so because there were many taverns to frequent and much addiction to drinking in all ranks of society. At this period universities were in a very rudimentary state. The idea of students living in colleges under college and university discipline was new and many students took unkindly to it, as some still do. King's College, Cambridge, had this to say about the problem:

> . . . after bodily refection through food and drink, men are commonly rendered the more ready for buffooneries and indecorous speech, and (what is yet worse) for detractions and quarrels, and for the perpetration of many other perilous misdeeds, paying then less heed to such-like excesses than when they are on a fasting stomach, whereby they oftentimes move the minds of other simple folk to quarrels, revilings, and excesses . . .

The college decreed that students should return to their rooms after meals except on special feast days when they could remain in hall 'for singing and

Ladies hunted occasionally on horseback but hawking, with the marlyon according to one list, was probably preferred

honest pastimes'. In addition no member of the college, were he fellow or student or anyone else, was allowed to hunt or fish or to keep dogs, nets, falcons, ferrets or to bring wild beasts into the college such as apes, bears, etc. The college was also careful to point out that it would not suffer damage to the fabric. No one should shoot arrows, or hurl stones, javelins, wood or clods within the college walls, and above all there must be no dice or other forms of gambling. It is not likely that these rules were generally kept.

For gentlemen not at university there was another important recreation, hawking or falconry. The elaborate order of hawks for gentlemen according to status will be dealt with in the next chapter. Here it is only necessary to record the importance of the sport and the pleasure a good bird gave its owner by its obedience and its hunting powers. The king's falconer held an honoured position in England, second only to his counterpart in France. Hawks gave status and were bought for large sums; J. W. F. Hill in *Medieval Lincoln* (1948) relates how Henry II's falconer went to Boston to buy Norway hawks, and that hawks were used to repay debts. Falconry was killed as a sport of kings, nobles and others by the invention of the hand firearm, but until sportsmen mastered the art of shooting birds in flight—and this was not until the eighteenth century—falconry persisted and was defended energetically by the old-fashioned as it is in the opening conversations of Isaak Walton's *Compleat Angler*. In the end only the hunter who cared for poetry in his killing preferred the hawk to the gun, which had all the advantages of sound and fury, allied to precision and the chance to display.

At home in the castle during the long winter evenings and on bad weather days, play was more peaceful. Women embroidered superbly. They also played chess, some as well as the men. The men wiled away the time eating and drinking, keeping their dogs fed and amused, looking at their horses and playing such games as lent themselves to gambling, backgammon being a

Draughts was one way of whiling away time at the castle

Everyone let off steam when it came to the dance

tanto mag ab eo prie. ut p obredra cone pseuri qua meidesinure emult lautanr:

renus uri. B alendas uras crolepi obutr ara mea. fra se molesta. L

favourite. They also practised the martial arts. There was a good deal of music from local and travelling minstrels, who also entertained with feats of balance, leaping and juggling. There was dancing too. There is a splendid marginal picture in a manuscript Bible of this period in the Bodleian Library of a very active dancing performance by a woman and a man. It is almost wanton in its abandon and not unlike the more extreme displays of modern dance. Altogether, within the castle walls and regardless of rank, there was in all probability a real sense of community and fun, with men trying the tricks and skills of the travelling minstrels and the women, more accustomed to bawdiness than their fine clothes suggested, joining in the laughter, the singing and the applause. On more restful occasions good stories were always enjoyed. At the start of this period, as Richard Barber relates in *The Knight*

22

and Chivalry (1970), the stories were probably about warrior knights and their audacious and bloody deeds; later, influenced by the troubadours, they were of chivalry and courtly love; and later still of fantastical, Arthurian adventures. It was quite, quite different from the lives of the cottars and villeins outside.

It was different also from the lives of Londoners. Strutt devoted one section of his book on English sports and pastimes to those who 'exercised in towns and cities, or places adjoining to them'. Even in his day (1801) he was thinking mainly of London, and probably in the twelfth and thirteenth centuries London, as always, was lucky in its amount of fun.

Information about it comes from William FitzStephen, a twelfth century churchman who was present at the murder of Becket in Canterbury Cathedral. He was remarkably percipient and took it for granted that men appreciated the value of physical exercise, of display and skill, of the desire to excel and act competitively, of the value of games, of man's need for cruelty and violence. And he linked these last characteristics firmly with man's desire to prove how valiant he would be in war. In his *Life of St Thomas* he described the London of his day, and introduced the subject of play with these words: 'Let us now come to the sports and pastimes seeing it is fit that a city should not only be commodious and serious, but also merry and sportful.'

On Shrove Tuesday, FitzStephen related, boys brought their cocks and were allowed to stage fights. The sport and the day were already traditional. The fighting-cock had been an emblem of courage for centuries and still had many years of glory to look forward to—the cock will enter the pits on many occasions in this book—and many regretted the law that banned him at the end of the eighteenth century. The boars 'prepared for brawn' also provided holiday fun when they were set to fight. Alternatively, bulls and bears were baited. Every Friday in Lent young men engaged in feats of war with blunted weapons; courtiers joined them to prove their worth.

It was not all violence but much of the fun was energetically physical. The boys after their cock-fights went off to the fields with an audience to play

Rounders, baseball, cricket? Whatever it was it confirmed the popularity of the ball

ball, some of them with clubs. In the Easter holidays water quintain, or tilting, was played in boats on the river. As the contestants had to stand up in boats propelled by oarsmen rowing forwards they often fell in, and FitzStephen commented, large crowds gathered on the banks and on the bridge 'to see and laugh thereat'. Summer was a time 'in the holidays' for leaping, dancing, shooting (with arrows), wrestling, casting the stone (with or without a sling) and 'practising their shields'. The girls tripped 'in their timbrels' and danced 'as long as they can well see'. Winter encouraged ice sports. Young men, 'striding as wide as they may', were sliding; others made themselves 'seats of ice, as great as mill stones' and were drawn across the ice by their friends and often fell together in a heap. They fought with poles, and some tied bones to their feet and with the help of a spiked staff propelled themselves across the ice as swiftly as 'a bird flieth in the air, or an arrow out of a cross-bow'.

In the smaller towns, scattered throughout the country, where the weekly markets were held, and in the bigger ones like Oxford, York, Lincoln and Norwich there were similar events. The markets brought in traders from a wide area and with them at the annual fairs would come the entertainers with their strange animals, their music and their feats of agility. In the villages rough games of football were already being played, one side against another or even one village against another village. The biggest matches were likely to be on Shrove Tuesday, but Sundays and holy days also gave opportunities for football, wrestling, boxing and primitive forms of bowls. Nothing that is known in more detail about play in the fourteenth and fifteenth centuries was wholly missing from life in the twelfth and thirteenth.

2

☆ MEDIEVAL DISPLAY ☆

Fourteenth and fifteenth centuries

Stokesay Castle near Craven Arms in Shropshire is a fine example of a medieval fortified manor house. It was built in the thirteenth century, on the site of two earlier houses, chiefly for a prosperous wool-merchant, Lawrence of Ludlow. Although to modern eyes it may appear comfortless, this type of house offered more privacy than rich men had previously known. Lawrence and his wife had an upstairs room to themselves (with observation windows on each side of the fireplace overlooking the great hall) and at the opposite end of the hall, also upstairs, was a room believed to be for women of the household to work and sleep in. In Lawrence's time there would have been very little furniture, and possibly his own room was also used for a courthouse—he was his own magistrate—or for receiving deputations of one kind or another. Nevertheless, in spite of the lack of furniture, the general appearance might well have been gay for it is probable that the walls were covered with tapestries of French or English manufacture, with other hangings and cushions of brilliant colours.

It was the beginning of a great period of display, when rich men began to make much of their surroundings and to regard war as an interruption best left to those young enough to enjoy it and to mercenaries they were ready to pay. In some respects, therefore, the play of this period was different. War games were less attractive and in their place the spending of money on appearances had a strong appeal. The colour that rich men brought into their homes they introduced also into clothing of great magnificence, proclaiming to all who looked upon them that English wool was best.

The pageantry of Stokesay was without doubt increased by the amount of entertaining a man in Lawrence's position was required to do. Hospitality in medieval times was expected, necessary, given and accepted. Merchants travelled far and without hospitality could not have conducted their business. They would bring with them pretty samples of the work of their own countries as presents for the ladies, they would entertain the household with stories of other lands and travellers' tales, and would join in the music and singing and dancing. They would eat and drink a great deal. In 1300 the language of communication was probably still French though later in the century English took over. All the women of the family would speak French as a matter of course and, as girls, would have learned housewifely duties, including the arts of entertaining, embroidery and dancing. Some of them would paint. The men, too, would speak French and those who had been put as pages in other great houses would have learned there to carve, and how to conduct themselves with ladies of their class, as well as the use of arms. They would also make the most of any singing voice they might possess and profit by an ability to play an instrument and to dance.

Outside, pageantry extended to the tournaments. At first, in the early 1300s, there was not much change: tournaments were still violent battles between opposing forces or individual contests which might lead to serious hurt or death. Gradually, however, the martial element disappeared, metamorphosed into stylized play. There was no longer uncontrolled fighting but combat under rules, still called a tournament, and jousting in the lists with lances across a barrier which divided one contestant from another. By the end of the fifteenth century knights were so heavily armoured that stronger horses, also protected and consequently slower, were needed to carry them. As spectacles these contests were very much enjoyed, but there was little danger. A less than perfect hit might unseat a knight who was picked up by his page with the loss of forfeit and his dignity, but generally it was the whole panoply with the accompanying sound of trumpets and banners flying that made the occasion. In popular imagination the affair to end all such affairs was the Field of Cloth of Gold. It was held near Calais in 1520 when Henry VIII met Francis I of France. Sumptuous temporary palaces were built and the jousting was only one of the many extravagances arranged for the gratification of the monarchs. Although this was not quite the end of the story very little importance was attached to jousting from then on and a few years later it was little more than an anachronistic holiday entertainment.

Jousting was for the nobility, to be watched only by others. Tilting at the quintain was anyone's sport in some of its many forms, while tilting at the ring could be used by those able to take part in jousting for practice in markmanship. The quintain was a target, and could be almost anything: sometimes it was a post, on more important occasions a shield, and Strutt records that occasionally it was shaped like a man, a Turk or a Saracen, indicating that the enemy at that time was connected in men's minds with the Crusades. The object was for the player, mounted or on foot, to score a hit with lance, if a knight, or stick on a central point. Sometimes, if the player missed the centre and hit the side, the quintain was so made that it would swing round, a projecting part taking a swipe at him to the joy of all. This was medieval humour of a regular kind and preserved for us at fêtes when the contents of a bucket of water descend upon the head of an unsuccessful competitor.

For townspeople pageants were growing very popular. They too were full of fun and colour. Pageants, more often than not, were connected with religion, as they still are in Catholic countries, and the best known pageants of medieval times were those of the cycles of mystery plays, to which further reference will be made. The pageant in origin was not a procession but a succession of individual scenes played on carts to audiences at certain points along a traditional route. At York today, when its cycle of plays is re-enacted by a huge cast of local amateur actors, some of the scenes are still played on carts. But medieval man thought pageants too much fun to be confined to religious occasions and they were used to celebrate state events, such as royal weddings, and soon became processions with tableaux on carts

The knights at the back are using their lances; those in front have broken theirs and are now using their swords. On the frieze below hobby horses and windmills

just whenever these could be justified or excused. They are still enjoyed today as the Lord Mayor's Show in London annually proves and as the modern carnival processions in many towns amply confirm.

Jousts, pageants and processions were all display and spectator sports. Other spectator sports on holy days included traditional, often pagan, seasonal mummeries and fertility rites. They would be followed often enough by feats of strength or wrestling matches, one of the most universal of all plays. Chaucer's miller, who at 'wrestling never failed he of the ram' (the prize), was one of many younger men throughout the country who sought personal satisfaction and admiration for his ability to throw his opponent in the ring. He had history behind him, for no sport had enjoyed such widespread popularity in the ancient world as wrestling, and it had been one of the Greek Olympic Games. Boxing likewise had an Olympic past, though in medieval times it survived only in its brutal aspects for settling quarrels or making new ones.

How far archery was regarded as a sport is difficult to say. Judging by the number of enactments which sought to reduce the amount of time 'wasted' on other sports when it might be spent in practice at the butts, archery grew less and less popular as the fifteenth century neared its end. Nevertheless it seems likely that those who excelled would always be eager to use their talent, and others would watch as men have always paused to watch demonstrations of skill. It is probable that there were local competitions and with them prizes, yet it is also understandable if archery was so much associated with duty and compulsion that many saw nothing in it that could be called play or fun. The long-bow was never a gentleman's weapon so it is not surprising that there is little information about its use except in war.

Times were changing as usual and only the conservatives and men in authority went on repeating their sermons and legal threats against those who frittered leisure away to the detriment of the defence of the realm. How conservatives as late as Edward VI's time felt about archery is splendidly told in a sermon of Bishop Latimer, often quoted in snippets but here repeated at greater length because it reveals much. Latimer was the son of a yeoman farmer.

> There is such dycing houses also, they say, as hath not bene wont to be, where young gentlemen dice away theyr thrift and, where dycing is, there are other follies also. For the love of God let remedy be had, let us wrastle and stryve against sinne. Men of England in tymes past, when they would exercise themselves (for we must needes have some recreation, our bodies can not endure without some exercise) they were wont to goe abroad in the fieldes a shooting, but now it is turned into glossing [cheating], gulling and whooring within the house. The Arte of Shooting hath bene in times past much esteemed in this realme, it is a gift of God that he hath geve us to excell all other nations withall, it hath bene Gods instrument wherby he hath geven us many victories against our enemyes. But now we have taken up whooring in townes, in stead of Shooting in the fieldes. A wonderous thing, that so excellent a gift of God should be so little esteemed. I desire you my Lordes, even as ye love the honour and glory of God and entend to remove his indignation, let there be sent forth some proclamation, some sharpe proclamation to the Justices of peace, for they doe not their dutie. Justices now be no Justices; there bee many good actes made for this matter already. Charge them

e Round Dance,
.eenth century,
.cursor of more
borate play of
same kind

Sóme courtoifis unvlla lumát ij regatdoit culo ij carollopxnt
a caivlle en mop eftaut. Il e Svus wiva la Svnes

upon their allegiance, that this singular benefite of God may be practised, and that it be not turned into bolling [cheating], glossing and whooring within the townes: for they be negligent in executing these lawes of Shooting. In my time, my poore father was as diligent to teach me to Shoote, as to learne me any other thing, and so I thinke other men did their Children. He taught me how to draw, how to lay my body in my bowe, and not to draw with strength of armes as other nations doe, but with strength of the body. I had my bowes bought me, according to my age and strength: as I encreased in them, so my bowes were made bigger and bigger: for men shall never Shoote well, except they be brought up in it. It is a goodly Arte, a wholesome kinde of exercise, and much commended in Phisick.

It was all far too late, as the ordinary man instinctively knew. The evolution of the hand firearm had begun a full century before Latimer's birth (c1485) and the comments of his younger listeners are not difficult to surmise. But apart from Latimer's anachronistic outlook, not unlike that of old cavalrymen who pleaded for the retention of horses in the army of World War II, there, in the sermon, is a pleasing picture of a young boy being taught to shoot. And he did appreciate the value of exercise, if not of play, and in so doing anticipated Henry Peacham who felt strongly about the matter one hundred years later.

On one other point Latimer was certainly right. There were 'many good actes for this matter already' which had not been enforced. They were passed in the reigns of Edward II, Edward III, Richard II, Henry IV, VII and VIII; and in 1477, in the reign of Edward IV, the Commons petitioned the king to make the law work. These acts are of interest to us because they list the games which were popular enough to warrant special mention as keeping young men from the butts: handball, tennis, football, hockey, dice, quoits, bowls, skittles and cock-fighting. Cards, which were introduced from France, Spain and Italy in the fifteenth century, were not included, probably because they were expensive to buy and used only by gentlemen. But they were soon as wicked as dice for promoting gambling. The naming of tennis is significant. The elaborate court game was probably not the game in the minds of the drafters of the act. There was a simpler ball game, the French *longue paume*, played across a net on any reasonably flat piece of ground; this was played with the hand, by several players on each side, and was a variation of handball, which was played against a wall. This kind of tennis was also played by gentlemen inside the courtyards of castles and fortified manors. The more elaborate game, still known as tennis or real tennis (not lawn tennis), was played first in monastic cloisters and later in buildings especially erected for the purpose. Handball was played by children and by all ranks of society. Basically it was the simplest game in the world: the bouncing of a ball against a wall with an opponent, the two players taking it in turns to strike the ball. In England it was also played against the church walls.

Throughout the history of play the Church was the champion of the poor. As the Reformation gathered momentum the puritanical element, but never the majority of churchmen, denounced play as a synonym for idleness. No one else believed it, except in the sense that play was unproductive and could therefore be allowed only in strict moderation to those who worked. In medieval times the church building was not sacrosanct. Many different events took place there because it was the only sizable meeting place; dancing in the churchyard was common; and as late as the eighteenth century Parson Woodforde was giving permission for the fives court against his church wall to be dug up, the implication being not that playing a game there was evil but that the court was unused. *

The acts in favour of practice at the butts were not always ignored. Joyce Godber in *History of Bedfordshire* (1969) picked out instances in the early sixteenth century of men being fined for playing: at Ampthill, in 1502, eleven men were fined twenty pence each for playing bowls and twelve pence for playing tennis. Six years later at Bedford there were fines for playing at cards. Miss Godber also recorded butts at Bedford for archery practice both north and south of the river Ouse. The manor court rolls of Leighton Buzzard contained a general prohibition of games, including tennis. One manor court decreed, in accordance with the law, that no boy must play at tennis while apprenticed, unless twelve years old, and even then only at Christmas.

Training enough men to reach the required standard to shoot for England was in fact a serious matter. A levy might be imposed at any time, when the required number of competent archers had to be found. So butts were everywhere, at quite small places—two in Hitchin, Hertfordshire, for

---

*This naturalness in church has continued in some places and is returning in others. To attend the service at Durham Cathedral on miners' day is to recapture a little of that relationship between God and man that medieval people took for granted. The service opens with colliery bands, one after the other, playing down the nave from the West door. They are each followed by their wives, carrying shopping baskets, and their children. In 1973 the preacher in a most successful address referred to the occasion as 'our picnic'.

example—and it was no wonder if men failed to associate shooting practice with play.

Of the other games mentioned in the acts bowls was as general as any. It had been popular for as long as man could remember for it was the easiest of plays to enjoy. The game was quickly set up, either by arranging wooden objects to be struck or knocked down with stone or ball from an agreed distance, or by placing an object on the ground and bowling in such a way as to get the ball or wood as near to the object (jack) as possible. The former game, the forerunner of modern bowling, was immensely popular in Germany during the middle ages, whereas the second developed most happily in England. The Dutch played a similar game on ice, later known as curling.

Skittles and bowling in alleys, if less popular than in Germany, was nevertheless encouraged by the growth in importance of the inn, serving the local community and the many travellers on the road. The authority of the innkeeper as a leader in his community could be considerable. He was described by Chaucer in the Prologue to *The Canterbury Tales* as bold in speech and wise and well taught. He often provided opportunities for play. Bowling greens followed the alleys, and the inn was the scene for 'meets' of fox- and other hounds. The innkeeper if he played his part well was, like the parson, a figure of importance to everyone.

Foxes were not yet the chief quarry of the hunt. The king's forest was diminishing but it was the hare now that was giving the greatest pleasure to those who pursued living things. The number of those who took part in the chase had increased and was to go on increasing as society accepted that there were others, merchants for instance, besides landowners who were important in the realm. The poor were still a long, long way from such delights, but the chase was in their blood also, and so was the desire to engage in combat with others. These two ingredients of man's nature appeared to find some satisfaction from the game called football.

Football had no common rules, and little restriction on methods used to get the ball, but it was clear that it was not permissible to carry a club. Gentlemen took no part in such a coarse exhibition of physical contact play, but a good many of them would watch and some would provide the field of battle, if it were not the kind of game that ranged over the fields between village and village or from one end of the town to the other. The object was to get the ball from one point to another by using the feet. The match could be between two sides of unequal numbers. Shrove Tuesday was a favourite day for an inter-village match, with all Lent in front of one to recover from the blows. G. G. Coulton in *Medieval Panorama* (1938) quotes a monk's disapproving opinion of football following a description of an incident at Caunton in Nottinghamshire:

> The Game at which they had met for common recreation is called by some the foot-ball game. It is one in which young men, in country sport, propel a huge ball not by throwing it into the air but by striking and rolling it along the ground and that not with their hands but with their feet. A game, I say, abominable enough, and, in my judgment at least, more common, undignified and worthless than any other kind of game, rarely ending but with some loss or accident, or disadvantage to the

players themselves. What then? The boundaries had been marked and the game had started; and, when they were striving manfully, kicking in opposite directions, and our hero had thrown himself into the midst of the fray, one of his fellows, whose name I know not, came up against him from in front and kicked him by misadventure, missing his aim at the ball.

And, as today, not always by misadventure. One man's opinion but still one likely to have been echoed by gentlemen throughout the country, especially by those in areas where feud matches between villages were becoming traditional. The match described took place in Henry VI's reign and the description is of particular interest because of the reference to marked boundaries. These would be natural features as they still were at Rugby School in the nineteenth century when the boundaries of play were explained to Tom Brown. This was probably not unusual but there were plenty of games, particularly perhaps in East Anglia, where play was across the flat countryside, and it was common also, as later, to play games of football in the streets.

Cock-fights were a compulsive enjoyment for many, and lasted in England officially until banned in 1795, and unofficially until the present. The origin of cock-fighting is sometimes credited to Themistocles who invited his soldiers to watch a natural cock-fighting in order to demonstrate that cocks fought not for gain or honour but from determination not to be beaten. Athenian law then decreed that a day a year should be set aside for cock-fighting. This practice was copied by the English, Shrove Tuesday being the traditional day.

Not surprisingly, Geoffrey Chaucer's works are as valuable source material as manor court rolls for illustrations of everyday behaviour. Chaucer frequently used a sporting simile. The carpenter's wife in the *Miller's Tale* was 'long as a mast, and upright as a bolt' (cross-bow bolt); the Summoner in the *Friar's Tale* was 'wood' (mad) 'as an hare'; he had also 'baudes' (procurers) 'as any hawk to lure in Engelond'; and he was more cunning in his ability to spy out a lecher for blackmail than any 'dogge for the bow, that can an hurt deer from an hool y-knowe' (he was better than a bow dog (today a gun dog) in telling the hurt deer from the sound or whole one). *

The Canterbury Tales can also be relied upon to reveal the kind of stories most enjoyed by castle and hostelry audiences, a mixture of bawdy, adventurous and romantic tales. They also make plain why authority had reason to distrust revelry. More even than today singing, dancing and drinking were followed by more wanton play. Chaucer's tales are full of that kind of merriment William of Malmesbury had in mind when he said (c1125) that the English liked revelling better than accumulating wealth, and that drinking parties often went on throughout the night. It is not difficult to see the twentieth century in Chaucer's stories: there is the carpenter's wife, a fair young thing setting her cap and singing very prettily, the miller blowing on his bagpipes, Perkin the apprentice victualler . . .

---

*That is, through his informers he was able to pick out victims for his blackmail who would pay him to keep quiet and not report them to the archdeacon.

> At very brydale wolde he singe and hoppe
> He loved bet the tavern than the shop.

And when Constance married King Alla in the *Man of Law's Tale* the guests enjoy themselves in the still customary way: 'They ete, and drinke, and daunce, and singe, and pleye.'

Even better than Chaucer's tales, from the point of view of the whole population, was the dramatization of stories to help the Church convey the Bible story to a mostly illiterate people. The Bible was in Latin (the Vulgate) and it was not until the sixteenth century that English versions were adopted in church. Meantime the people had to be taught. The Church's efforts in dramatization began very early, before 1066. On the most important dates of the Church calendar pictorial representations would be made of the events commemorated. Probably the earliest performance showed the Resurrection. Gradually these dramas grew in power and popularity throughout the Catholic world. When the imagination had been thoroughly fired the people took over the mystery plays through the craft guilds and these, with miracle and morality plays, were of outstanding importance in adding a new dimension to man's play.

Most people when coming across the mystery plays for the first time are startled by their broad humour and naturalness. They illustrate what has almost been forgotten in modern times, that medieval man saw his nature whole; nothing was compartmentalized, and fun was not excluded from religious life. The forty-eight plays of the York cycle were performed by the representatives of forty-eight guilds, beginning with the Barkers who handled the Creation and the Fall of Lucifer and ending with the Mercers and Judgment Day. There were similar arrangements for the Towneley (Wakefield), Coventry and Chester cycles. The plays were not acted in a

Mystery and miracle plays were staged on carts at different points in a town. This one is said to be at Coventry

theatre but on carts moving to various points about the town. Strictly, miracle plays were not Bible stories but about saints, and represention of these plays may have remained with the Church. Morality plays, which came later, were more sophisticated. They were chiefly for castle audiences, played probably by professionals and not unlike the well-known one in Shakespeare's *Hamlet*.

Singing was a major enjoyment everywhere. Ballads telling a story were popular, and many of them were spoken with musical accompaniment from the harp or guitar as they might be today at a folk festival. Often they were about romantic figures or gallant gentlemen like *King Estmere* whose tale has been put to music by Gustav Holst in modern times:

> Hearken to me, gentlemen,
> Come and you shall heare;
> Ile tell you of the two boldest brether
> That ever borne were.
>
> The tone of them Adler Younge,
> The tother was Kyng Estmere;
> They were as bolde men in their deeds
> As any were, farr and neare.

Or they told of love, like that of Clerk Saunders for Margaret:

> Clerk Saunders and may Margaret
> Walk'd owre yon garden green;
> And deep and heavy was the love
> That fell thir twa between.
>
> 'A bed, a bed,' Clerk Saunders said,
> 'A bed for you and me!'
> 'Fye na, fye na,' said may Margaret
> 'Till anes we married be!'

Perhaps the ballads at the inn were sometimes less chivalrous. Chaucer's miller would have had his own versions.

There was a great difference between the music heard at the beginning of this period and three hundred years later. Instruments in the thirteenth century—animal horns, simple pipes and flutes—were so primitive that they were scarcely regarded as capable of making music on their own. Out of the Crusades, however, came the discovery of instruments common in the Arab world, and soon they were being played by minstrels at castles, manors and at fairs: a kind of violin called a vielle; the tabor, a small drum; the lute; the rebec, another form of fiddle; the shawm, like an oboe with double reed; the trumpet; the citole, a stringed instrument; and drums. For many years it was difficult to imagine what the sound of medieval instruments playing together was like; recently there has been a welcome revival of interest in making and playing these instruments and there is now an opportunity for everyone either to go to concerts or to hear recordings. Parallel with secular music, which included martial tunes as well as accompaniments to singing and the gradual development of solo playing, there was a great advance in church music, the Church being the most influential patron of all. A good minstrel

There were many musical instruments in the later middle ages, singing and playing being much enjoyed

Practice made perfect even in those days, the performance being all the better for musical accompaniment as now

was expected to play several instruments and to sing, but by the fifteenth century professional string players were taking the place of the minstrel. New music was being composed and a new profession, that of composer, created. Music-making at the coming of William I to England was perhaps the least regarded part of play; by the time of Henry VIII it was highly valued even by monarchs who excelled at vigorous sports as well.

The more important nobles of the fourteenth century had their jesters to keep them amused, their minstrels to play and sing to them and, from time to time they would entertain strolling players who would act a play, dance, sing, juggle, and perform feats of agility called tumbling. All over the world acrobats and jugglers had enjoyed popularity for centuries. They were to be found in China, Egypt, Greece and Rome. They had performed acts in the ancient world which were, in so far as it is possible to judge, fully the equal if not superior to those of modern times. Their descendants in skill were welcome everywhere, not least at the fairs.

It was at the fair that the working man got his chance to see fresh faces, new sights and indulge in fun and laughter. The fair was an important concession granted by the king. Usually a fair lasted three days and probably there would be two fairs each year in a market town. Both fairs and markets were for trade but whereas the market attracted, as it still does, nearby traders and customers to satisfy weekly wants the fairs, especially the big ones, brought merchants, traders and entertainers from all over the country and some from the continent as well.

Fairs were often in the first place granted to the local church and fell usually on some feast day in honour of a saint. Grant of a fair brought with it the right to close shops in the town to ensure that the tolls exacted were as many as possible and the trade concentrated in one place. Cambridgeshire, for example, had fairs in twenty-four towns and villages and in nine of the twenty-four there were two fairs each year. An outstanding Cambridgeshire fair was St Awdrey's at Ely but even so it could not rank with Stourbridge fair which was the greatest in the country and dated from 1211. Thousands of packhorses were said to have converged upon Cambridge for this fair which lasted three weeks. At it college bailiffs would lay in all those commodities for better living that could not be obtained at other times of the year. Wholesale merchants would come there especially to meet each other and to arrange deals.*

With the arrival of all these wealthy people and a huge congregation of buyers and sightseers the entertainers moved in. Theatrical performances at Stourbridge were very popular and the university authorities are said to have viewed the happenings at the fair with distrust and apprehension. The minstrels were there, of course; so were the jugglers and the tumblers. Here, too, came the luckless bear on his chain, destined to be baited by the bravest local curs, and if there was an oddity, like a bearded woman, it was sure to draw large crowds. As Trinculo said when he discovered Caliban (*The Tempest*), 'Were I in England now, as once I was, and had but this fish painted, not a holiday fool there but would give a piece of silver: there would

---

*Other great fairs included St Bartholomew's, St Ives, and Winchester.

*t was dogs who
eeded pity; they
were expendable,
the bear was not*

this monster make a man; any strange beast there makes a man; when they will not give a doit to relieve a lame beggar, they will lay out ten to see a dead Indian.' Everyone pressed forward to see a strange sight; the rich man in his castle and the poor man at his gate had a common curiosity, which was certainly not confined to the medieval period. For the rest, there was bound to be cock-fighting, dicing and all forms of gambling, singing, dancing, drinking and quarrelling, as the court records reveal—and in fact everything that is now associated with the closing hours of a holiday and a crowd on a fine summer's day.

It is not difficult to find evidence for the play that satisfied the violent and physical sides of man's nature even in medieval times; it is much less easy to discover where and how often medieval man was able to indulge in more tranquil pursuits. It is known that fishing was a regular sport for of all the literature that is famous on this subject none is better known (except Isaak Walton's) than *The Treatyse of Fysshynge With an Angle* (1496), the second part of the *Boke of St Albans* believed to have been written by Dame Juliana Berners, the prioress of Sopwell, Hertfordshire. It is clear that the rights of fishing and fowling were usually reserved for the benefit of those living in big houses; nevertheless there must have been many areas where there was opportunity for the poor to fish without being in constant danger of arrest on charges of poaching. To some extent there is support for this view from Dame Juliana who adds a few words of Christian admonition in her treatise: 'Ye that can angle and take fysshe to your pleasures as this forsayd treatyse techyth and shewyth you, I charge and requyre you in the name of alle noble men that ye fysshe not in noo poore mannes seuerall water, as his ponde, stewe, or other necessary thynges to kepe fysshe in wythout his lycence and good wyll.' The passage seems to suggest that it was not unknown, after a poor day, for a fisherman to improve the look of his catch by lifting a fish or two from another man's pond, where he kept supplies for the benefit of his larder. But Dame Juliana clearly understood the value of fishing as a sport, for she claimed that it should be undertaken principally for 'solace and to cause the helthe of your body, and specially of your soule'.

If there were other ways in these centuries of achieving solace and health they are hard to find. No one would walk for pleasure but some might ride for solace. Occasionally, too, some might swim, although Sir Thomas Elyot in his book *The Governour* (1531), while recommending the exercise, thought there was 'perile in the lernynge therof' and in his opinion it had not been much practised in recent times.

Indoors there were peaceful things to do if the place lived in was secure. The majority had not that good fortune in the country and in their tiny dwellings were satisfied if they could keep evil out and warmth within. Life was not comfortable in the Middle Ages and even in the castles and the manor houses it must have been hard to find the warm, quiet corner for a game of chess. Nor was the countryside inviting. Men were full of superstitious fears and unless one was able to move about in the company of others it was best to keep close to home. By the end of this period towns were increasing in importance and in population and there is a temptation to see in them a description of the nation's way of life. But this is far from being the case. Towns were centres of big populations but most people for many centuries yet were to live outside them.

3

☆ INTERLUDE ☆

Instruments of medieval play

The horse, the hawk and the dog were all status symbols in medieval times. They revealed instantly to ordinary people the rank of a stranger and determined the response he received when asking the way. Chaucer in his prologue to *The Canterbury Tales* was careful to point out the mounts of his pilgrims. The Knight and the Squire had good horses, he implied: the Monk was important: 'ful many a deyntee hors hadde he in stable'; the Clerk from Oxford, on the other hand, had a horse that was 'as lene . . . as is a rake'; the Wife of Bath sat easily upon 'an amblere'; the poor Parson went 'afoot' always in his parish; the Ploughman rode upon a mare; the Reeve 'sat up-on a ful good stot', while the Merchant, who needed more than anyone to make his position clear, sat 'hye on hors' wearing a Flemish beaver hat and with his boots fastened rather elegantly.

The Ellesmere manuscript illustrating Chaucer's The Canterbury Tales *shows the squire and the merchant on lively horses, the Wife of Bath on a solid one and the reeve, the clerk and the miller on animals more befitting their stations*

Apart from the value of a good horse for war, or for getting about, the horse played a prominent part in hunting and enlivened the life of nobles from the earliest times with its ability to race and the opportunity this gave for gambling. Emotionally there was and is a great bond between horse and man, expressed in an eighteenth century edition of the *Encyclopaedia Britannica* in these words: 'The horse, in a domestic state is a bold and fiery animal; equally intrepid as his master, he faces danger and death with ardour and magnanimity . . . he exults in the chase; his eyes sparkle with emulation in the course.' Words that a medieval king or noble would have read with approval. One discovery made in the course of the Crusades was that the Arab horse was much lighter, quicker and more manœuvrable than the animal bred in Western Europe. However, it could not displace the heavier horse at once for it was incapable of carrying an armoured man, particularly as the horse had to wear some armour itself. How many horses were in the country at this time is impossible to compute but it must have been an enormous number if Froissart's accounts of the combined operations of war and hunting in France are to be believed. Edward III's company in France were all mounted and Edward himself, according to Froissart, had sixty couple of stag-hounds, and as many hare-hounds. He hunted with the hounds or hawks on most days. So did many of the nobles with him, using their own dogs. Froissart personally reported that Gaston, Earl of Foix, had 600 hunting dogs in his castle.

There were many kinds of dog. John Caius, who refounded Gonville Hall at Cambridge in 1557, wrote a short treatise in Latin entitled *Of English Dogs, the diversities, the names, the nature and the properties*. It is an engaging work, full of information about the 'gentle kind, serving the game'. They were called English dogs because 'we are more inclined and delighted with the noble game of hunting; for we English are addicted and given to that exercise, and painful pastime of pleasure'. Caius went on to say that since 'chasing the beast' (hunting) and 'taking the bird' (fowling) are the two most important pastimes for gentlemen there are necessarily two kinds of dog for these purposes: 'one which rouseth the beast and continueth the chase; another which springeth the bird, and bewrayeth the flight by pursuit.' The first kind, called *venatici*, were divided into five sorts: 'The first excelleth in perfect smelling (the Harrier, the Terrier and the Bloodhound); the second in quick spying (the Gazehound); the third in swiftness and quickness (the Greyhound); the fourth in smelling and nimbleness (the Tumbler and the Thievish dog which at the mandate and bidding of his master fleereth and leereth about in the night).' Long descriptions were given by Caius of each dog, all expressed in the most laudatory terms. The dictionary definition of a tumbler is a lurcher, like a small greyhound; but Caius said 'flowing first of all out of the French fountain', meaning originally a French dog.

The second kind of dog, for 'taking the bird' or 'serving the hawk' was known as a spaniel by 'the common sort of people' but, said Mr Caius, they should be divided into dogs for the falcon, dogs for the pheasant and dogs for the partridge. Moreover, other spaniels 'findeth game on the water', and there was a special dog, the setter, which was also very good for fowling ('my meaning is, of the partridge and the quail'). 'When he hath found the bird, he

These dogs, in George Turberville's famous The Noble Arte of Venerie and Hunting, *are classified as blacke hounds, dunne hounds and whyte hounds*

keepeth sure and fast silence, he stayeth his steps and will proceed no further; and with a close, covert, watching eye, layeth his belly to the ground, and so creepeth forward like a worm.'

Caius referred to a third kind of dog, non-sporting but used for the play of women; it was called the spaniel gentle, or the comforter. He was not very kind about it. The dogs were 'sought for to satisfy the delicateness of dainty dames, and wanton women's wills, instruments of folly for them to play and dally withal, to trifle away the treasures of time, to withdraw their minds from more commendable exercises, and to content their corrupted concupiscences with vain desport. A silly shift, to shirk irksome idleness!' And he added for good measure that the smaller the puppies the more their mistresses loved to bear them 'in their bosoms'. Strutt in his *Sports and Pastimes* had some different names for dogs including descriptive ones such as butcher's hounds, dunghill dogs and pryckereard curs, but these, it would appear, were all mongrels.

Dogs were also included among the many performing animals. These unfortunates, as most of them probably were, travelled the fairs and

Making a monkey take the place of a man to put another animal (here a bear) through its tricks has never failed to amuse

performed at castles and in the streets. They were trained to 'talk', to dance and to perform a variety of tricks, as they had been for centuries, and their antics were shared with the horse. An intractable horse was sometimes used for baiting, but on the whole English people preferred to see the bear or bull treated in this way, the horse being a friend of man. All kinds of animals—bears, cocks and, according to report, a hare—were used for performing tricks including the popular one of beating a tabor or drum. Favourites, as usual, were apes and monkeys, always good for laughs and ready to co-operate in copying man by riding on the backs of other animals or wearing his clothes. The same performances today would still appeal.

King John was said to be so fond of good horses, particularly running horses for races, and dogs that he would accept them in lieu of fines. Nevertheless the prices they fetched fell far below those of the best hawks, which were well-nigh worshipped and protected by punitive legislation. Nobles going to Church left their horses outside but took their dogs and hawks in with them. * There was a pecking order for hawks commensurate with the rank of their owners. It read: for an emperor, the eagle, the vulture and the merlin; for a king, the ger-falcon, the tercel of the ger-falcon; the falcon gentle and the tercel gentle for a prince; the falcon peregrine for an earl; the bustard for a baron; the sacre and the sacret for a knight; the lanere and the laneret for an esquire; the marlyon for a lady; the hobby for a young man; the goshawk for a yeoman; the tercel for a poor man; the sparrow hawk for a priest; the musket for a holy water clerk; the kestrel for a knave or servant. The accuracy of the list may well be questioned for Brian Vesey-Fitzgerald has written in more general terms of the peregrine gentle, the gyr-falcon and the goshawk being reserved for the gentry and Sir John Paston, it will be remembered, got into a great fuss about his goshawk (*The Paston Letters*). But there was no doubt in medieval times about the importance of the subject. A statute of Edward III stated that 'every person which findeth a

---

*Others took their pets. There is a record of nuns being admonished for taking birds, rabbits, hounds, and 'suchlike frivolous things' to church. This is perhaps less surprising than it may sound to townspeople. At evensong in Ludlow during the late summer of 1974, two dogs were among the congregation and were said to be regular attenders.

Faulcon, Tercelet, Laner or Laneret or other Hawke, that is lost of their Lord' must 'bring the same to the Sheriff of the County', and the sheriff was to make proclamation in all the good towns of the county that he had a hawk in his custody. Even if the hawk was not claimed, the finder, if he were a 'simple man' did not get the bird back but he did get a reward; if he were a 'gentleman' he got the hawk and was obliged to pay boarding fees to the Sheriff for the days it had been kept. The penalty for not giving up a lost hawk was two years in prison and the price of the hawk. A poor man could not hope to pay the fine so, theoretically, at least, he continued in prison for ever. Hawks and hawking were for gentlemen only and mostly they hunted with men only in attendance. Occasionally, there was a ladies' day, as there was for hunting, when efforts were made to make it easier for the ladies to kill.

As for the victims of the chase they, too, had their positions in society, higher it might seem than those of human villeins. The stag fitted well into medieval ideas of hierarchy. He was so obviously a noble animal and rightly regarded according to the thought of the time, as aristocratic enough to play his part in the king's pleasure; the deer qualified because they were beautiful

...wks could be even more ...pensive than horses and ...re much prized and ...tected

...e stag, the hounds and ...e huntsman would not be ...ually in such close order

and the boar, when found, because he was courageous. The hare just got a place because his cunning and running were admired. The fox, at this period, was not praised. He was vermin and permission to hunt him and the cony was frequently given to the king's tenants and later on to tenants of other lords; sometimes Poor Wat the hare was included in the permission as a borderline case.

Conies were netted; so too were birds, including songbirds, and the fox was often trapped. There was small thought in all this of animal husbandry and agriculture: the king and barons were not interested in such lowly subjects. Their passion was for the preservation of enough game to ensure their fun. Of the birds pursued by hawks the heron came at the top of the list as the quarry most suitable for the attention of kings and nobles; however, any strong flying bird would do for the pleasure of showing off a hawk's undoubted skill.

The English have always had a reputation for finding cruel sports irresistible. Cocks, bulls, bears and dogs have been the greatest sufferers. All classes have enjoyed these spectacles of animals seemingly fighting for their lives against each other. One of the cocks in a fight was almost certain to be killed by the end of the day, and the dogs—curs and expendable—chosen to attack the bulls and bears were usually badly hurt. Bears were too valuable to their showmen to be severely injured, but bulls were often unlucky: they were due to be slaughtered anyway and were required to entertain the public before being despatched. Many men kept fighting-cocks for the pleasure of boasting about them, just as boys boast about their conkers. In a number of ways tribute is still paid to the popularity of cocks and cock-fighting. 'That beats cock-fighting' is still a common expression, so are 'that cock won't fight', 'a cock-shy', 'to live like fighting-cocks', and perhaps 'a cock and bull story', referring to the fanciful stories men tell about their favourite sports.

Among the instruments used in medieval play were the arms, or military weapons, that were so important for the defence of the country that their proper use was encouraged in mock fights and practice at the butts. In 1181 the Assize of Arms listed, according to their rank, the weapons that freemen were bound to possess, including swords, shields and spurs. In the fourteenth and fifteenth centuries authority was obsessed with fear that young men would neglect their practice with the long-bow. All household-ers, below the rank of those permitted to bear arms, were required to have a long-bow and arrows in the home. They were not permitted to have cross-bows or hand-guns. Fathers, or others in authority such as masters of apprentices, were required to see that boys from the age of seven learnt to shoot with the long-bow and to practise with it on holidays. Strutt recorded that round-headed arrows were used in forest areas to protect the venison from harm. As long as authority remained convinced that the country's security depended on the long-bow, practice had to be regular; for it was known that England's enemies, who relied on mercenaries to do their fighting, found the cross-bow to be more accurate in inexperienced or unpractised hands. The bow, usually the cross-bow, was in regular use in the hunting field to despatch the quarry and it was also used for cock-shooting,

Poor cock: probably his performance in the ring or pit had been cowardly. Now he was paying the penalty

presumably the same kind of sport as the cock-shy, a way of despatching birds that had shown little courage in the pits or ring. Other weapons used for sporting combat were staves in place of swords, especially for fencing.

By far the most important tools for play, in these centuries as well as all others, were the ball, or ball substitute, and the clubs, bats and sticks invented to propel the ball further or more swiftly from one point to another. It took thousands of years for the ball, in all its manifestations, to become the near perfect object for its purposes that it is today, but that never mattered much to those who enjoyed the play it supplied. Greeks and Romans played with balls; so did the Persians who are said to have been playing polo at least as early as 500 BC. Balls were commonplace in the Middle Ages. They were made of wood for bowling, of pigs' bladders for kicking around, of pieces of cloth rolled together and stitched in a round, or of pieces of leather stitched to form a hollow round, which was then stuffed tight with almost anything resilient: cloth, feathers, hair or wool.

Almost all the ball games played today can legitimately claim an ancestry from the distant past. The basic games with balls are throwing and catching them, bowling them, hitting them with clubs and kicking them. All these things were done as far back as history is able to record and it says much for the importance of play that man has not only seized his opportunities always to use the ball in these ways but has created dozens of games out of his ingenuity for enjoying himself, using any object that was to hand for improving the sport, and even manufacturing obstacles and complications to increase the fun.

Part of medieval man's ingenuity was used in improving his clubs, a not very surprising development considering the time spent in manufacturing weapons. He soon had more serviceable sticks and bats, tapered and curved to suit his needs, and targets to aim at, and pins to knock down in bowling. More important, he made use of buildings for games in which he bounced his ball against the walls, and he invented a net to play across and scratched marks on the ground to denote areas of play.

All the same it seems surprising that a ball game as complicated as tennis should be evolved in the Middle Ages and particularly that it should become so popular. There is something to be said for the view that such a game could not have been invented had not groups of intelligent young men, good no doubt at chess, been shut up together in monasteries with too little to do. Undoubtedly it satisfied a desire for physical exercise while offering an incentive to win by guile.

There seems no room to doubt that the game originated in the monasteries of France. No castle had those features of the cloister, including the penthouse roof, that were necessary to the game and were copied in the courts especially built for tennis by Francis I of France at the Louvre, Paris and by Henry VIII at Hampton Court, both in 1530.* The names still used in England and America, as well as France, to describe the hazards, dedans and tambour for example, confirm its French origin which Albert de Luze in his authoritative work, *La Magnifique Histoire du Jeu de Paume*, sets out beyond dispute. In de Luze's opinion tennis was first of all a game enjoyed by young priests, and it is easy to imagine them larking about together with a ball, using the sloping roofs of the cloisters and the gaps between the pillars to help in the defeat of an opponent. When the lines called yard marks (chases) on the floor were added is not known. There are many references to the game in the fourteenth century and to players. In England ladies watched, but there is a delightful portrait, thought to be fourteenth century, of a French lady about to bat a ball with a club. It is also known that in the thirteenth century France had many ball-makers and that later balls were imported into England. Shakespeare was not wrong when he described tennis balls as a possible present from the Dauphin to Henry V:

> We are glad the Dauphin is so pleasant with us;
> His present, and your pains, we thank you for:
> When we have match'd our rackets to these balls,
> We will, in France, by God's grace, play a set,
> Shall strike his father's crown into the hazard:
> Tell him, he hath made a match with such a wrangler,
> That all the courts of France will be disturb'd
> With chases.

From the French name for tennis it is clear that the game was played originally with the hand (*jeu de paume*) and only later with the racket. Then for a long time it was played either with the racket or with the hand as in the many games of handball (fives) played against walls, sometimes buttressed and giving an angle and thus more interest or variety to the play.

But tennis was played across a net, a simple cord with tassels hanging from it to indicate if the ball went under and not over. In Erasmus's *Familiarum Colloquiorum Opus* (1524) Nicholas and Jerome argued about the rival merits of hand or racket play.

---

*The Hampton Court tennis court is one of the oldest in existence (1530). There are still quite a number of modern courts in England, France and the USA where the court was copied and notable champions born. The best opportunity for the public to see a court is at Lord's Cricket Ground. It is in the building opposite to the members' entrance at the back of the pavilion.

Real tennis as it used to be and very nearly still is. Probably the most complicated game ever developed to make use of every obstacle in the players' surroundings

NICHOLAS: No play is better to exercise all parts of the body than a game using the hand: but that is fitter for winter than summer.

JEROME: There is no time of the year with us but what is fit to play in.

NICHOLAS: We shall sweat less if we play with the racket.

JEROME: Let us leave nets to fishermen; the game is prettier if played with the hands.

Fives players argue like Jerome even today, but no one attempts to play tennis with the hand or with more than two players on each side, as was certainly done in the sixteenth century.

It was an American historian of tennis, Malcolm D. Whitman, a great player of lawn tennis, who applied himself to the problem of the evolution of the racket in his book *Tennis: Origins and Mysteries*. It was an appropriate title, for some of the mysteries still remain. In his opinion the bare hand was first covered with a glove, then bound with cords to improve the stroke, for with the fingers bound together the hand formed a bat. Next a wooden bat like a wooden spoon was used; then the bowl of the bat was hollowed and parchment stretched across it;* and finally parchment (used for many years for battledore and shuttlecock) was abandoned in favour of stringing with intestines or gut. Strung rackets with short handles appeared in several sixteenth century pictures but the date of stringing might easily have been earlier. Other historians are not ready to agree with Whitman, thinking that stringing may have been suggested first by the insertion of a stick into a

---

*Robert W. Henderson of the New York Public Library who compiled the bibliography to Whitman's book used to say that many valuable manuscripts had been lost because they were used in this way.

bunch of cords. * Henderson dated the start of tennis in France between 1150 and 1200 and mention of the racket came in Chaucer's *Troilus and Criseyde* (1385): 'But canstow playen raket, to and fro . . .'

So, in spite of the unorganized state of most popular games, special areas were set apart for tennis, chiefly because, no doubt, it appealed strongly to the right people, kings and nobles. It was played very early in closed areas, some cloistered with penthouse roofs and some just straight low-walled courts. Probably it was the enclosed game that was known as *jeu de paume* and the game across a net without boundary walls as *la longue paume*. In England both were referred to as tennis.

Besides tennis there was another recreation, bowls, played in bowling alleys and on grass, and capable, therefore, of being played in private as well as elsewhere. Grass was the easier because houses were beginning to have lawns.

The tranquil play of fishing was slower in development as far as its main instrument the rod was concerned. This was of short length, manufactured, it would appear, from the hedgerow by the fisherman himself. Hazel shoots of about two years' growth were recommended. There was no reel and this, with the shortness of the rod, must have made playing a fish difficult. Perhaps fishing, in spite of its popularity, was curiously unscientific in most areas, but Dame Juliana startles modern readers in her treatise on fishing by describing artificial flies, many of them closely resembling the ones in use now. She said that the pleasure of the sport lay in seeing fair, bright, shining-scaled fishes on the bank, deceived by the fisherman's crafty means. Strutt, on the other hand, had nothing to say about fishing because in 1801 (he remarked untruthfully) it was the same as it had always been.

At the close of the fifteenth century it seemed likely that some games would not have to wait long for rules and regulations which would govern play and make contests more equal. Jousts and sword play, fought with lighter weapons now that armour was fast disappearing, had elaborate observances which were acceptable to all those taking part. Balls for tennis and bowls were being manufactured and to some extent standardized, as were rackets. It was not hard to make up acceptable rules for bowling at jacks or pins. But there was still a great difficulty, not to be resolved until the nineteenth century, and this was the shape and size of the playing areas. Games played against or with the help of walls were nearly all controlled by local circumstances; Henry VIII and Francis I later set standards of measurement for tennis courts and these were copied by the rich, but open air games, mostly enjoyed by the poor, continued to make do with anything that was going for a long time yet.

---

*The author has put forward elsewhere the theory that the hand bound in this way was the origin of the word 'fives', used later for boxing as in the phrase 'a bunch of fives'.

4

Sixteenth century glamour

If any one man set the pace and raised the standards of play in the new century it was the king, Henry VIII himself. Medieval in courage, cruelty and ruthlessness—qualities which served him well in politics—he was nevertheless a Renaissance man in other important respects. He was educated and appreciated learning. He had style. Everything he did was brilliantly colourful. Like his daughter Elizabeth, he easily commanded the support of his countrymen in the face of foreign threat. He was loved for his arrogance, for his performances in the hunting field and for his keenness for tennis and bowls. The fact that he danced well, played instruments, sang and composed made everyone feel that whatever activity they chose the king might be doing it as well. In the words of Professor G. R. Elton: 'He gave his nation what it wanted: a visible symbol of its nationhood.' In the town at least, and in London in particular, he led a swashbuckling, display-loving aristocracy in the direction they wished to go, and without losing control. Strong, coarse, immoral and brilliant were the characteristics of many at the

Henry VIII helped culture along by including music among his attainments. The other person is his jester

top—and they rubbed off. By Elizabeth's time there were many groundlings who had enough contact with their betters to feel an integral part of an exciting society. It was heady stuff.

Love of display was obvious. Dress in Elizabeth's time was so fantastic as to be unbelievable. The critics were severe; there were puritans about and they knew that this was idle play. William Harrison, in his famous description of Elizabethan England for Holinshed's *Chronicles* (1578), quoted Andrew Boorde, physician and traveller, as saying that anyone trying to describe an Englishman's dress was forced in the end to draw 'the picture of a naked man, unto whom he gave a pair of shears in the one hand and a piece of cloth in the other, to the end he should shape his apparel after such fashion as himself liked', since he could not find any garment that would please anyone for any length of time. Harrison added that 'this phantastical folly of our nation', from the courtier to the carter, meant that one day it was the Spanish guise that was the fashion, the next the French, then perhaps the Turkish manner, or Morisco gowns and so on. 'Nothing is more constant', he commented, 'than inconstancy of attire.' He was not the only one not to mince his words. Fynes Moryson, another traveller, said the English outdid the Persians. Parsons and playwrights denounced and lampooned. * What was so remarkable was that so few escaped the fever: the butcher, the baker and the chandler all dressed up and it was difficult if not impossible to tell a wig-maker from a courtier. The women, less surprisingly, did their best to prevent the men from stealing all the sartorial splendour and one of the best comments of the time was the description of a woman wearing a farthingale and a tight doublet as 'a trussed chicken set upon a bell'. The colours were equally capricious, again according to Harrison, the ladies sporting 'goose-turd green, peas-porridge tawny, popinjay blue, lusty gallant and such like'.

The men's clothes were set off by another extravagant play, that of carrying swords and other weapons. Again everyone was doing it. If a man was too poor to swagger along with a rapier at his side and a hand itching to draw in the expectation of a quarrel over nothing, he could at least carry a dagger in his belt. Schools of fencing for gentlemen were run by Spaniards and Italians. The Italians were the more fashionable because everything Italian was fashionable. There was a craze for it. Letters Patent were issued in 1540 to a society known as the London Masters of Defence and these Masters remained prominent members of society up to the Civil War.† Sword play had greatly changed in a hundred years from the time when the broad sword had to make a dent in an adversary's armour and a buckler was used to parry blows. Now the rapier and the thrust were the weapon and manner of delivery. There were books on fencing by this time but only one in English, a

---

*MALVOLIO: She did commend my yellow stockings of late, she did praise my leg being cross-gartered. (*Twelfth Night*)

†In the eighteenth century it was the 'gentlemen' prize-fighters who ran schools for that other noble art, boxing, and from that date onwards the sports and games professionals, if good enough, found themselves honourable and enviable positions in the refuges offered by many of society's élite, provided they were associated with the kind of play that appealed to such people, eg horse racing and cricket.

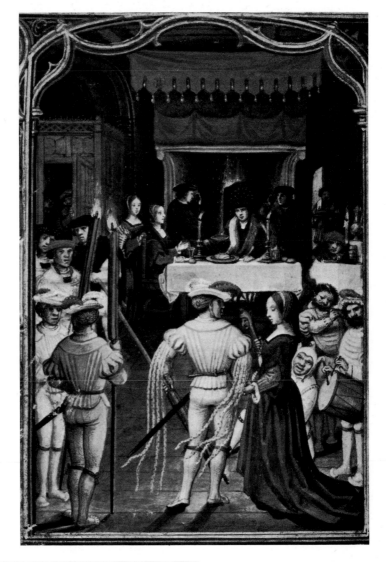

Feasting was part of everyday life for the rich and not to be hurried. Minstrels and jesters provided entertainment

A paisants Woman riding upon the

66

Not a grand lady but a peasant woman in her finery off to market

translation. Fencing was liberally mentioned in the work of dramatists and it was not only Shakespeare's Prince of Verona who wanted to shout 'Rebellious subjects, enemies to peace' when confronted by brawling in the streets (*Romeo and Juliet*).

The fashionable gentry and the people also shared the delights of bear-baiting and cock-fighting, now elevated to the rank of show business for there were pits as well as theatres on the South Bank and elsewhere. FitzStephen in the twelfth century described how the 'natural heat' of the magnates who rode out to watch young men play had been stirred by the strenuous activities of 'unbridled youth'. Now it was stirred again by the brutalities of cock-fighting, and the sight of huge bears fighting against the hounds let loose among them. The only difference between the twelfth century and the sixteenth century was that these sights were now regular entertainments to be enjoyed weekly, or even more frequently; and to the excitement had been added the fascination of organized gambling.

Good views were provided at the pits from scaffolding erected for the benefit of the spectators. Thomas Platter, a German traveller who had much to say about English ways in 1599 (he approved of the civic pomp) thought cock-fighting and bear-baiting well worthy of detailed record. He was sufficiently interested after the bear-baiting to go round to the back to see 120 mastiffs in an enclosure and also 12 large bears and several bulls. It is useless to feel censorious. All but a very small group enjoyed these spectacles, and although Elizabeth I was not to be found on the scaffolding of the South Bank, special baitings were arranged for her and good Elizabethans described the scene of these vicious affairs as 'sweet entertainment', 'very pleasant to see' and 'laughable'. John Stow said (*Survey of London*, 1598): 'those who go to Paris Gardens, the Bell Savage or Theatre, to behold bear-baiting interludes or fence play, must not account of any pleasant spectacle, unless first they pay one pennie at the gate, another at the entrie of the scaffold, and a third for quiet standing', not unlike, it may be thought, the arrangements for League football matches today. The law gave strong support to these entertainments for the justices were required to ensure that no plays were performed on Thursdays and Sundays to protect the organizers from too much competition.

The violence of the times and the extraordinary pleasure gained by these robust Elizabethans from watching pain and misery inflicted on captive animals extended to public hangings of fellow human beings. Some of these events, if the criminal was notorious enough, created carnival scenes. One such was the hanging of William Hacket (1591), the religious fanatic who wanted to dethrone the Queen. At his execution in Cheapside he stirred emotion to such an extent that the crowd became barbaric in its fury but exhausted and quiet enough when justice had been done, and been seen to be done.

Inflicting pain seemed to be in everybody's nature (and it is no doubt just below the surface today). Children suffered almost as badly as animals for education was enjoying a period of popularity among parents and few of them considered that Greek and Latin could be taught without a more than liberal use of the rod. This subject would be outside the boundaries of this book were it not for an extraordinary volume entitled, *The Scholemaster or the Plain and Perfite Way of Teachyng Children to Understand, Write and Speake in Latin Tonge* (1570). The author, Roger Ascham, was one of the best scholars of the period and incidentally one of the most enthusiastic defenders, at this late date, of the long-bow. He wrote about it passionately in another famous book, *Toxophilus*. In *The Scholemaster* Ascham, holding views that were commended four hundred years later, drew this comparison between what was regarded as work and what was regarded as play: Play, he said, was doing what a man liked in the way he liked, and he suggested that the methods of play could be adapted to learning. He wrote:

> It is part of the Divine Providence of the World, that the Strong shall influence the Weak, not only on the Battlefield and in Diplomacy but also in Learning and Literature.
>
> Fond schoolmasters, neither can understand, nor will follow this good counsel of Socrates, but wise riders, in their office, can and will do both: which is the onlie cause, that commonly, the young gentlemen of England, go so unwillingly to school, and run so fast to the stable. For in very deed fond schoolmasters, by fear do beat into them, the hatred of Learning, and wise riders, by gentle allurements, do breed up in them, the love of riding. They find fear and bondage in schools, they feel liberty and freedom in stables: which causeth them, utterly to abhor the one, and most gladly to haunt the other.

Ascham praised good pastimes. It would be foolish to suppose, he said, that he was against them, for even at his age he still used all exercises and pastimes that were fit for his nature and 'habilitie'. He listed what he considered to be gentlemanlike pastimes; for learning, he thought, should always be mingled with 'honest mirth' and 'comlie exercises'. These exercises were riding, tilting (still popular, as Stow also said), to shoot fairly with the bow and surely with the gun, to vault, to run, to leap, to wrestle, to swim, to dance, to sing, to play instruments, to hawk, to hunt, to play at tennis and to take part in all pastimes which involved labour in the open air and in the daylight, which were suitable exercises for war and peace. Presumably he included bowls, now being played on bowling greens with

Rings for bull and bear baiting on the south bank of the Thames

biased balls and, if he had thought of it, curling which in Scotland already was played with brooms for sweeping the ice. A Pieter Bruegel painting of an ice scene showed a game in Holland in the sixteenth century. Brooms were in use.

Ascham's advocacy of practice with the long-bow probably reflected his own past skill with it, but others agreed with him that the long-bow was still a military weapon. As late as 1591 the Queen was yet willing to express the view that archery was not only good recreation but important for the defence of the realm. She recognized that some now had guns although it was right once again to prohibit bowls, dice and cards so that archery might flourish and all those connected with the trades supplying the equipment might not starve. Unemployment was a serious problem at that date, and Elizabeth feared violence. There were a great many sturdy beggars wandering around to every good citizen's unease.

The Beggars Act of 1598 emphasized the apprehension felt about those who travelled around in an uncontrolled way; traditionally it included those engaged in the entertainment industry.

> And be in further enacted . . . that all persons calling themselves scholars going about begging, all seafaring men pretending losses of their ships or goods on the sea going about the country begging, all idle persons going about in any country either begging or using any subtile craft or unlawful games and plays, or feigning themselves to have knowledge in physiognomy, palmistry, or other crafty science, or pretending that they can tell destinies, fortunes, or such other like fantastical imaginations; all persons that be or utter themselves to be proctors, procurors, patent gatherers, or collectors for gaols, prisons, or hospitals; all fencers, bearwards, common players of interludes, and minstrels wandering abroad (other than players of interludes belonging to any baron of this realm, or any other honourable personage of greater degree, to be authorised to play under the hand and seal of arms of such baron or personage;) all jugglers, tinkers, pedlars and petty chapmen wandering abroad etc. etc. including all such persons not being felons wandering and pretending themselves to be Egyptians, or wandering in the habit, form, or attire of counterfeit Egyptians [gypsies]; shall be taken, adjudged and deemed rogues, vagabonds and sturdy beggars . . .

and punished accordingly. There was nothing very new about most of this except perhaps the protection for players of interludes under the patronage of important personages. An Act of 1383 had been concerned with vagabonds and beggars and the Tudors constantly returned to the problem and tried to solve it. The Beggars Act of 1495 had included restrictions on apprentices, servants of husbandry, labourers and servant artificers, none of whom were to be allowed to play at tables (backgammon), tennis, closh (a kind of croquet), dice, cards, bowls or any other unlawful game except at Christmas in the home of or under the supervision of his master. * The Act of 1536 had specifically enlarged on 'palmistry, or other crafty sciences, whereby they bear the people in hand [deceive] that they can tell their destinies, deceases,

---

*Christmas had always been regarded as a special period of relaxation even in the Paston's time (1400s) when times were equally hard. Normally it was jocund but Lady Morley after the death of her husband said 'there were none disguisings, nor harping, nor luting, nor singing, nor none loud disports; but playing at the tables, and chess, and cards.'

and fortunes . . .' It was all a great worry particularly at a time when few, even at the head of society, were free from superstition, and when, moreover, the dissolution of the monasteries and the enclosures of common land had greatly increased the problems of feeding the needy poor. (Odd to look back to an earlier time when one of the accusations against monks was that they kept too many dogs and other animals, thus depriving the poor of alms.) Nevertheless the difference between making Acts of Parliament and enforcing their provisions was as usual great. Entertainment went on and itinerant players learnt to know the places where they were likely to be brought before the justices and punished according to the law. Curiously enough the penalties provided another form of entertainment for the people, for the offender was usually placed in the stocks or whipped naked at a cart's tail through the streets.

Although times were hard it can be assumed that the usual fun was enjoyed on Sundays and other holidays. There was football, which Philip Stubbes, a puritan, reported on in 1583, his account being even more scathing than that of the Caunton chronicler two centuries earlier. It was a 'bloody and murdering practice' rather than a play or recreation:

> For doth not every one lie in wait for his adversary, seeking to overthrow him and to pick him on his nose, though it be hard stones, in a ditch or dale, in valley or hill or what place soever it be he careth not, so he have him down . . . So that by this means, sometimes their necks are broken, sometimes their backs, sometimes their legs, sometime their arms, sometime one part thrust out of joint, sometime another, sometime their noses gush out with blood, sometime their eyes start out, and sometimes hurt in one place, sometimes in another. But whosoever scapeth away the best goeth not scot-free, but is either sore wounded and bruised, so as he dieth of it, or else scapeth very hardly. And no marvel, for they have sleights to meet one betwixt two, to dash him against the heart with their elbows, to hit him under the short ribs with their gripped fists, and with their knees to catch him upon the hip, and to pick him on his neck, with an hundred such murdering devices. And hereof groweth envy, malice, rancour, choler, hatred, displeasure, enmity and what not else; and sometimes fighting, brawling, contention, quarrel picking, murder, homicide and great effusion of blood, as experience daily teacheth.

An exaggerated, prejudiced account, perhaps! It is necessary to pick one's way through such opinions, even those of scholars, to make a personal judgement on the recreations of the period. Ascham, for example, listed the pursuits of gentlemen, and they read like those of knights in the age of chivalry or like the sports at public schools in the nineteenth and early twentieth centuries as described by Sir Cyril Norwood. Latimer, preaching again, painted a completely different picture. Attacking the prelates and through them the rest of rich society, he said, 'Ever since the prelates were made lords and nobles the plough standeth; there is no work done, the people starve. They hawk, they hunt, they card, they dice; they pastime in their prelacies with gallant gentlemen, with their dancing minions.' And later, in the same sermon, he asked, 'Who is the most diligentist bishop and prelate in all England . . .? I see you listening and hearkening that I should name him . . . It is the Devil . . . He is never out of his diocese.'

It has to be admitted that by this time some gentlemen appeared to have made play the whole of their culture. In earlier times it had been war and play; now war had receded as a pursuit, and when a Queen who appreciated adulation and pageantry sat upon the throne there was opportunity for sophisticated men, who were also politicians, to indulge freely the different aspects of their natures, the coarse and the cruel, the love of display and sweet dalliance. So a day at a cock-fighting session or bear-baiting might be followed by an evening's music, stately dancing, or composing poetry: a classical moment in some men's lives when they actually controlled their play by indulging a natural propensity for alternating currents of enjoyment. It was also recognized, as Christopher Morris has pointed out, that 'the arts were social accomplishments when accomplishment could open many doors'.

Under these circumstances it was not surprising that in the country hunting maintained its elevated position in the eyes of society. Gervase Markham, who wrote a discourse on horsemanship in 1593, maintained in a later book *Country Contentments* (1611), that the recreation of hunting was 'most royal for the stateliness thereof, most artificial for the wisdom and cunning thereof, and most manly and warlike for the use and endurance thereof'. The same feeling of stateliness was evident in George Turberville's work: *The Noble Arte of Venerie or Hunting* (1576). If additional support were needed for this view it came from the Queen herself: she hunted when she could and added even more enchantment to the scene.

But the forest was receding. The fiercer kinds of wild animal had been hunted to extinction or had moved north. The plough was taking over. Hunting was changing and the hare, which, it is tempting to believe, appealed to the Elizabethan mind because of its tortuous cunning, was becoming a firm favourite for the chase. The deer was still pursued with enthusiasm but the fox had not yet achieved its present unenviable pride of place. How Reynard might have thought about it had to wait for John Masefield to relate four centuries later but poor Wat, the hare, had a more illustrious scribe. *

> By this, poor Wat, far off upon a hill,
> Stands on his hinder legs with listening ear,
> To hearken if his foes pursue him still:
> Anon their loud alarums he doth hear;
>   And now his grief may be compared well
>   To one sore sick, that hears the passing bell.

Part of the 'fun' of hunting the hare was that on the open heath he remained in sight for so long:

> He cranks and crosses with a thousand doubles
> The many musets through which he goes
> Are like a labyrinth to amaze his foes.

Two centuries later, John Byng (Lord Torrington), a thoughtful, intelligent

---

*From *Venus and Adonis* by William Shakespeare.

Both feet off the ground: Queen Elizabeth and the Earl of Leicester giving the lead to the evening's enjoyment

Royal progress: it was expensive entertaining Queen Elizabeth for she did not come alone

man, who understood that some people believed the sport too cruel, defended his love of this particular play.

Like other monarchs before her, Queen Elizabeth undertook Royal Progresses. Because she was a vain woman, and because the age was what it was, these events which had always been costly to the hosts were now cripplingly high for all but the richest courtiers. It was more than enough for most owners of big houses to have to feed the retinue; now entertainment on the most lavish scale had to be devised. It was on one such visit, when she was staying with Lord Montague, that a diversion from the sumptuous revels was created by placing Her Majesty comfortably on a chair in the park whence she could shoot (with a cross-bow) at the deer behind a pale in their paddock. She killed three, and the Countess of Kildare one. Later on that year, 1591, she was at Elvetham, staying with the Earl of Hertford. Stupendous preparations were made for her visit, including the building of extra rooms. This time part of the quieter entertainment was an open-air, hand-ball tennis game, which she watched for an hour and a half. The men played 'stript out of their dublets', 'five to five with hand-ball at bord and cord', an occasion which gave rise to Strutt's unlikely derivation of the word 'fives' from this source. Queen Elizabeth was reported to have enjoyed herself. She watched from a window, below which they 'did hang up lines, squaring out the forme of a tennis-court'. All ten players came from Somerset and were presumably of exceptional physique and fame.

Everywhere Elizabeth went it was taken for granted that she wanted to be sung to, recited to, and played to. They played to her while she was shooting the deer at Lord Montague's place. The most elaborate entertainments were devised for her, the most gastronomically imaginative meals served to her, and life for her on these visitations was full of expensive surprises. The masques performed were always elaborate and excessively complimentary; they had big casts and were the equivalent of modern stage and film spectaculars. Poetry flourished under these conditions and, if it was sometimes bad, it probably did not matter much if the sentiments were sound. Sometimes the whole phantasmagoria ended with the bangs of fireworks, a new and exciting toy. Inside the house there was probably a relatively new amusement, billiards, but there is no record of Elizabeth having played it.

The newest amusement, and the most triumphant, of the Tudor period was the theatre, an opportunity for men who wrote well and/or excitingly to attract audiences to their dramas. These were performed by the Queen's Men, the Lord Chamberlain's Men and other nobles' Men, who were protected by the patronage of those whose livery they wore. In spite of the liveries they earned their own livings and several became the first actors (all men) to make reputations for their performances. On a lower social level troupes of actors played in inn yards. The London city fathers hated the theatres, bracketing them with cock-fighting pits as places where misbehaviour was almost sure to occur. They banned them from the city, but The Rose, The Swan and The Globe, all famous theatres dating from 1576, were beyond the boundaries, either in Shoreditch or on the South Bank. These theatres were public. They were open-air auditoriums, the performances taking place in daylight from a stage nearly surrounded by the audience, which included men and women of all classes. The private, closed theatre with evening performances in candlelight for superior persons (in rank but not necessarily in manners) came a little later. Meantime the city fathers were not far wrong. Comedy was broad and suggestive either in the words or the actions, the battles fierce. The actors took the members of the audience into their confidence with soliloquies and asides and the audience was probably quick to respond. Nevertheless, some of the dramas were remarkably dull and must have relied on the actor's 'business' and the bloodshed for a hearing.

Plays were not always in theatres; often they were in inn yards

It was just remarkably good luck that Marlowe and Shakespeare were among the actor-authors writing and able to exploit the audience's taste for historical dramas. These gave Shakespeare, in particular, plenty of practice in craftsmanship before he presented his major tragedies in the new century and in front of more sophisticated customers. However, Shakespeare never wrote a play that had such success among his contemporaries as Thomas Kyd's *The Spanish Tragedie*. From the 1590s it was played again and again, and was well spoken of in revivals for fifty years. It was a powerful play of action and cunning.

Music and dancing prospered exceedingly in the Elizabethan period, although the break between court and popular culture came much earlier in these arts than in other recreations. There were many composers and most of

The Globe theatre scene of many Shakespearian and other Elizabethan playwrights' plays

them were concerned with music for the lute, virginals, organ and viol. The madrigal was a unique contribution of the age. Based on Italian models it was nevertheless so transformed that it became a wholly English style, much practised at court and in country houses. In general the people were divorced from these enjoyments. They were still at the pipe and tabor level and their appreciation of other instruments was associated mainly with martial music. It was much the same with the dance. The vigorous jigs of the country had given way at court and in other places of fashionable society to elegant manœuvrings which matched the splendid clothes. However a romp was still enjoyed and that great piece of showmanship, Kemp's Nine Days' Wonder, performed in a dance from London to Norwich in 1600, no doubt enchanted nearly everyone. Kemp set down his own account of his 'Morrice' to Norwich to counter the lying of the ballad-makers. And a very good job he made of it. 'My setting forward was somewhat before seven in the morning, my Tabourer struck up merrily, and as fast as kind people thronging together would give me leave, through London, I leapt!'

Cecil Sharp, who spent much time at the beginning of this century making a collection of traditional dances, called Kemp's effort 'a very un-Morris-like escapade', and rightly so for the morris-dance as now interpreted is a ritual performed by men only at specified times of the year, eg in Spring, and on May Day. It is a spectacle, whereas the peoples' folk-dances are social, like the maypole and the chain dances, and are about communal rejoicing and the mating of boy and girl. A few of these dances have survived in their old forms, the Cornish floral or furry dance for example, and can be enjoyed by anyone; others have been rescued by folk song and dance societies all over Europe.

In a sense it can be said that the sixteenth century closed with Englishmen in towns accepting, without conscious appreciation of what was happening, that the short experiment of being one community in play had come to an end. In the country the division had always been there, because the holding of land bestowed playing privileges that were jealously guarded, while the rough and tumble ways of the poor on holiday were not recreations as a rule for gentlemen. In the towns it had been different, partly because the different gradations of the middle class bridged the gap between the top and the bottom and partly because the gentlemen living in towns were less isolated from their fellow human beings. As FitzStephen related, gentlemen came to watch others play and then decided to show that they could compete. The pageants, too, were unifying spectacles because all enjoyed them. Now town society was changing. Everywhere schools were being founded for the sons of middle-class parents and, for so long as part of the community were educated while the rest were left in ignorance, there was no chance of creating a single culture, even in play. The story of the next three centuries concerns that division; the story of the twentieth century tries to show what happens to play when a nation offers full-time opportunity for education to all.

5

☆ *DIVISION* ☆

Seventeenth century changes

It was not only Bishop Latimer who had felt strongly about the play-loving ways of Tudor society. The puritans, a growing body of influential townspeople, had been equally upset by the greedy, self-indulgent citizens they had seen all around them. Now, after the death of the old Queen (1603), they came more and more into the open, to express their own views and, with growing strength perhaps, to lose all sense of proportion. Latimer had never suggested that play was a sinful waste of time; the puritans did, or rather they regarded it as idleness which in itself was sin. Play therefore became the whipping-boy for the deeper divisions which were to exist for a century between the supporters of the king and court and the hard-working business and merchant class whose disciplined domestic life was so much at variance with the cavalier ideas of a good time.

Nothing in the world of play highlighted the division more dramatically than the developments in the theatre. For a short time men and women of all social groups, except the puritans, continued to mix in the open-air theatres, seeing the same kind of plays, and often the same plays, as they had done in the previous century. Gradually, however, the cavaliers deserted the open air for the new rectangular indoor theatres which were private to those who could afford to pay. The new stages were a great advance on the old ones, for painted scenery could now be used (instead of placards indicating FOREST) and there was the additional advantage of playing in artificial light which encouraged illusion. For the puritans these theatres were soon recognized as the habitations of the Devil and, given their point of view, who could say they were wrong? As early as 1578 John Stockwood had said in a sermon, speaking then of the open-air theatres, 'Will not a filthy play, with a blast of a trumpet, sooner call thither a thousand, than an hour's tolling of a bell bring to the sermon a hundred?'

And there was that other divider of the old theatre audiences, the intellectual content of the new plays. Many of the plays now were written for a minority group, not all broad humour and noise and tumult, but subtle comment on one section of society. The young playwrights, led by Ben Jonson, were disinterested in the crowd; they liked an audience that could react to satirical treatment of London life.

Ben Jonson was a favourite at court for the masques he wrote: gorgeous, poetical spectacles with speeches, sometimes enlivened by the introduction of satirical interludes between the acts of the masques. From this kind of entertainment John Citizen and his wife were usually excluded, as they were from the modern plays about illicit love and intrigue, played in the private

Plays were now being printed and read by those who were captivated by the theatre

theatres with great success, particularly when they were written by Beaumont and Fletcher. In the same way the generality of townspeople missed the so-called horror tragedies which brought in, gratuitously if need be, scenes of torture and pain for the special purpose of satisfying those who got a thrill of pleasure from witnessing them.

By 1618 the argument between king and puritans had reached such a pitch that King James I issued a Declaration to his Subjects concerning lawful sports to be used, commonly referred to as *The Book of Sports*. It was a clever document because at face value it was nothing more than a liberating declaration designed to protect the people's right to play; actually, as all knew, it was a political bolt aimed at the puritans. The preamble made plain that the King was not prepared to have his wishes opposed by either papists or puritans, who were punishing 'Our good people for using their lawful recreations and honest exercises upon Sundays and other Holy Days, after the afternoon sermon or Service'. The King, in the previous year, had rebuked 'some Puritan and precise people' in Lancashire for prohibiting play but it was now evident to him that a more general declaration needed to be made. Two evils, he said, resulted from the puritan attitude: first, men were turned from the Church because it allowed no honest mirth or recreation; secondly, ordinary people, denied the opportunity to make their bodies fit for war, spent their leisure in the ale-houses with filthy tiplings and discontented speeches. The question was then asked: 'When shall the common people have leave to exercise, if not upon the Sundays and Holy Days seeing they must apply their labour, and win their living in all working days?'

His Majesty's pleasure was, therefore, that after the end of Divine Service everyone should be allowed to enjoy lawful recreation, dancing (either men or women), archery for men, leaping, vaulting, or any other such harmless pastimes; and further, in season, they should be allowed to have May games, Whitsun ales and Morris dances and set up maypoles and have customary sports. (Church ales, sometimes at Easter and sometimes at Whitsun, were days of special almsgiving to the parish church, in return for which strong ales were brewed and drunk.) Nevertheless, there was to be no bull-baiting on Sundays, nor interludes (comic scenes introduced originally between the acts of mystery plays) and 'at all times, in the meaner sort of people by Law prohibited, Bowling.' Bowling took place at the ale-houses and was usually accompanied by too much drinking. Those who failed to attend service were prohibited from going to the said recreations.

However stimulated by political considerations the Declaration was, it remained a fact that James was interested in sport. Although it was Charles II, after the Restoration, who earned the sobriquet 'Father of the British Turf,' James, long before he came to England from Scotland, had sponsored horse racing. Now, under the enthusiastic lead of the Duke of Buckingham, among other things Master of the Horse, James made racing the sport of kings and,

It looks like a maypole painted in suburbia by a seventeenth century Lowry

The kill. The prince is being handed the knife to despatch the deer if it so pleased him

that the Prince or chiefe (if so please them) do alight and take
assaye of the Deare with a sharpe knife, the which is done

in consequence, a pre-occupation of the cavaliers surrounding him. Naturally they organized it in the interests of their class; it would not have occurred to them to do otherwise as horse racing already had a long history and horses capable of racing belonged only to them. The difference between the old days and the new Stuart period was that racing became a studied sport with greater attention given to breeding and to courses. For the first time Epsom and Newmarket became names on the racing calendar.

James himself had no one particular sporting passion, except perhaps for hunting. Rather he was versatile, in spite of his poor physique, indulging in anything that passed time away. Perhaps he was seen in a slightly more favourable light than usual on a visit to Lincoln, described in Sir F. Hill's *Tudor and Stuart Lincoln* (1956). By 1616, Lincoln, one of the most important medieval towns, had fallen on bad times. James was sorry; he thought Lincoln deserved a better fate and was willing to support a scheme to open and scour the Fosse (the Roman canal) giving Lincoln access to ports. On his way to Scotland the following year he decided to visit the city. He hunted along the heath from Grantham and after all the ceremonial of reception he spent eight days in the city 'cocking at the George by the Stonebow, fencing at the Spread Eagle and hunting on the heath'. He enjoyed himself and no doubt his visit to Lincoln gave the city a lift, if it did not further impoverish it. One year later steps were taken to preserve the game and wild fowl about Lincoln and Ancaster heath for the King's sport. There were other attractions, the bull-baiting and the horse racing were both good. This was a common method of progress for the King. He is heard of again hunting along the heath, fine hare country, on the way from Baldock to Royston in Hertfordshire.

One noble lord described in a sentence the cavalier's existence: 'We eat, and drink and rise up to play and this is to live like a gentleman', a fair summary of quite a number of lives in that peaceful period before the Civil War. Fynes Moryson, the traveller, noted that the Englishman had given up his old bad habit of quarrelling and drawing his sword in the street at the slightest provocation. Instead, he recorded, he travelled abroad to enrich his mind and study letters. John Earle, Bishop of Salisbury, held a different opinion. In his view 'a young gentleman of the university' was one who came

Real tennis again and a clearer picture of the court with its hazards. This is a picture of a game, Jeu de Paume, *in France, 1632. Today the net still sags in the middle but in a less pronounced way*

there just to wear a gown and to be able to say that he had been to such a place; his father, on the other hand, was satisfied if it proved true that the best fencing and dancing schools were there and his son showed proficiency at tennis and found a good tavern. John Brinsley, who wrote a book about the Grammar School (1612), worried about the extent of play. It should be moderate: 'Clownish sports, or perilous, or yet playing for money are no way to be admitted'; games took a boy's mind off his work. Robert Burton, in that remarkable investigation of man's nature *The Anatomy of Melancholy* (1621), quoted Paulus Jovius, an Italian historian of the sixteenth century, as pointing out that the English nobility lived in the country so much, making 'too frequent use of it, as if they had no other means but Hawking and Hunting to approve themselves gentlemen with'. Burton's view was similar. The reason why melancholy attacked so many European nobles was that they did not know how to spend their time except in playing and, he said, like the Frenchman would rather lose a pound of blood in a single combat than a drop of sweat in honest work.

Burton was a meticulous workman himself so it is useful to know his choice of pastimes that were popular. In his list hunting and hawking get first mention, but, he said, some men enjoyed fowling just as much whether it was with guns, lime, nets, glades (a net hung across an opening), gins, strings, baits, pitfalls, pipes, calls, stalking horses (a horse trained to enable a fowler to conceal himself behind it), setting dogs, coy-ducks etc. He continued with fishing, surprised that gentlemen were willing to wade out up to their armpits but remarking that the thought given to fishing with the variety of baits, artificial flies and so on made it the more commendable; further, it was 'still and quiet'.

Burton's list of sports and games included tennis, then ringing, bowling, shooting, keelpins (a different arrangement of pins from ninepins), trunks, quoits, pitching bars, hurling, wrestling, leaping, running, fencing, mustering, swimming, gardening, wasters, foils, football, balloon, quintain etc. All these were the play of country people. The gentlemen rode races on horseback and had wild-goose chases on horses and many of them were inclined to 'gallop quite out of their fortunes'. In another section he mentioned dancing, singing, mumming, stage plays, and agreed with the King's Declaration supporting May games, wakes and Whitsun ales. He saw no reason why the people on these special occasions should not feast, sing and dance, have their puppet-plays, hobby horses, tabers, crowds, bagpipes and other instruments, play at ball, barley breaks (Strutt said that this game depended on fleetness of foot) and whatever they liked best. All the same it was important that games should remain refreshments and not become a way of life as they were for so many gentlemen.

Indoors, Burton regarded chess as 'a good and witty exercise' for the right kind of man, but cards, tables and dice were better left alone for they were usually put to evil purposes and 'tis money that flies'. Best of all was to walk amongst orchards, gardens, bowers, mounts and lawns, for Burton had donnish ideas of play; for him the best pastimes were quiet ones, not so vigorous that they might upset a train of thought at the back of his mind; to be honest, study was the best way of dispelling melancholy. Interestingly enough, for it showed how far a new pursuit was prospering, he included gardening as suitable for gentlemen. He was not recommending physical exertion, only the planning of large gardens and perhaps the propagation of plants. In this he was following Francis Bacon who had included a delightful piece on gardens among his essays. Bacon, also, was thinking of 'prince-like gardens not under thirty acres of ground'. That was in the sixteenth century and by the seventeenth no gentleman's country house could be without a garden, especially as Charles I was employing the Tradescants, father and son, those sedulous collectors and importers of plants. A tradition had been established that over the years would be extended to all classes, even to people who could manage nothing larger than a window box.

Burton's lists made it clear that gentlemen now had a full complement of pastimes to satisfy all their emotional needs. They had the excitement of the chase, the violence of the cock-pit, the tranquility of fishing and gardens and even social, sexual play in the masques. Many tried to make the ingredients of play into a recipe for life. Some appeared to succeed; others, if Burton was right, did not, for melancholy still crept in.

The rest of the population had little opportunity for melancholy. A possible exception was the yeoman farmer: for so long as he retained contact, as he did in some areas, with his lord, he was not wholly excluded from gentlemen's play. Where contact was lost he was soon deprived of his remaining independence and had to settle down with his fellows to play only on statutory and church holidays. Remarkably, it was the end of the long-bow as a weapon of war that finally demoted him from an assured position in society; he might regain it temporarily as one of Cromwell's Ironsides but generally he became of little account for a long time. Apart from him, the poor had more or less fun according to the circumstances. It was hard to come by in puritan areas but still there were reports all over the country of cock-fighting (for three years, 1634–36, it took place in Knotting Church, Bedfordshire, on Shrove Tuesday and was then stopped as unseemly), bull- and bear-baiting, wrestling, stool-ball (favoured in the north), football (Hine, the historian of Hitchin, related that there was a football close there, as there was in nearby Baldock, but that men still preferred to play in the streets), bowling, board games at the inns and also billiards, dice for gambling, fives or some kind of handball against convenient walls, tennis over a string in the open and, on festival days, running and leaping. Entertainers continued to travel around and probably soon learned to by-pass puritan areas. Hine confirmed that such areas could show courage and determination: in 1630 the people of Hitchin informed the Master of the King's Hawks 'that they would no longer suffer a levy for the Royal birds'. The King kept his hawks and hounds in the area and was often around. The puritan victory had its gloomy side, however, for all forms of play were restricted for the townspeople.

The great leveller of society, when the winter was cold enough, was the ice. For rich and poor alike it was irresistible. There was a great frost in 1608, well reported in a dialogue between a Londoner and a countryman visiting the capital to see the Thames frozen over in a pamphlet entitled 'The Great Frost. Cold doings in London, except it be at the Lottery.' The countryman

The Dutch made great use of the ice for fairs and games. Here they enjoy a game of golf

remembered the Thames being frozen over in the fifth year of Elizabeth's reign, * so it was an uncommon occurrence. As might be expected it was the 'wild youths and boys' who first tested the ice, but eventually everyone was on it, playing football, shooting at pricks (targets) and, in one illuminating sentence about human nature, 'the citizen's wife that looks pale when she sits in a boat for fear of drowning, thinks that here she treads as safe now as in her parlour'. Among the amenities on the ice was a tavern.

In more normal years the regular places for skating were north of London and in the fens and the lowlands of Scotland where curling was a regular sport. It was Dutch influence that encouraged Englishmen, and New Englanders in America, to make the most of ice as a playground. In Holland, everything that happened in London in 1608 was an annual commonplace. Many Dutch paintings show fairs on ice and every relevant enjoyment.

---

*The Thames was wider and shallower in the seventeenth century. The Buckingham Watergate in the Embankment Gardens at Charing Cross shows where boats took on their noble passengers at that time.

69

6

☆ *INTERLUDE* ☆

Puritan spoilsports

Professor Hudson writing on puritanism in the fourteenth edition of the *Encyclopaedia Britannica* described a puritan as 'a spiritual athlete, characterized by an intense zeal for reform, a zeal to order everything—personal life, family life, worship, church, business affairs, political views, even recreation—in the light of God's demand upon him'. If this was so it is not difficult to understand why he rejected Elizabethan society together with the middle-course politics adopted by the Queen and the outrageous extravagances and moral looseness of the court. He was still more opposed to Stuart attitudes of kingly arrogance, once he understood what the doctrine of Divine Right meant; and faced with the external evidences of cavalier carelessness and pleasure-seeking idleness he had no option but to resist their influences upon the people. Nevertheless when it came to play there was every degree of opinion between the extreme views of puritan zealots on the one side and the King on the other. Many men who were to espouse the King's cause had no patience with the London court set and believed that they did a disservice to the King and his party; many men who were to fight with Cromwell enjoyed their own recreations and had no real objection to King James's *Book of Sports* or to its reaffirmation by Charles I in 1633. Charles had in fact gone further than James by adding to the original document these words: 'of late in some counties of our kingdom, we find that under pretence of taking away abuses, there hath been a general forbidding, not only of ordinary meetings, but of the Feasts of the Dedication of the Churches, commonly called Wakes'.* Charles wanted these feasts to be observed and he commanded the justices of the peace and of assize to make sure that lawful sports were everywhere allowed. Probably the new declaration made little difference; it would be ignored in strong puritan areas and keenly supported where sporting squires ruled.

Of more importance, especially in the capital after the start of the Civil War was the ordinance of 2 September 1642 which closed the theatres officially and put an end to public recreation. This time it was the puritans' turn to find a decree difficult to enforce. Raids on theatres for failing to close were numerous and ultimately there was another ordinance designating all actors as 'rogues'. This was a leaf taken from the earlier Beggars' Acts, in effect

---

*Wakes had been important for centuries and for centuries they had been controversial. Nominally they celebrated the birthday of the parish church and were an evening gathering of parishioners for a feast and merriment. Often, according to critics, the merriment got out of hand. There was also trouble when men and women from other parishes joined in for the drinking. Many fairs began as parish wakes.

extending the penalties reserved for strolling players to resident ones. Views and attitudes were so mixed that it is helpful to recall that Milton, who held strong puritan opinions, in 1634 had his masque *Comus* set to music by Henry Lawes, a courtier, and performed at the Earl of Bridgewater's castle in Ludlow. And certainly not by accident, for Lawes suggested the idea to Milton, who knew Lawes to be a member of the Earl's household. The occasion was the Earl's appointment as Lord Lieutenant of Wales.

The extreme puritan view of the theatre was loudly publicized by William Prynne, not a likable man but a courageous one of considerable learning. His vitriolic *Histriomastix: the Players Scourge or Actors Tragedy* (1632), in the most immoderate language attacked the theatre as the source of many evils. It was not only the plays with their immoral sentiments and the actors with their wanton behaviour (including dressing up as women, for women were still barred from appearing on stage although they took part in private masques) that were at fault, but the audience as well. The theatre, he thundered, appealed to all lusts; attracting the idle gallant, the tittering citizens' wives, the pickpockets whose trade remained a prosperous one in spite of severe penalties if caught, and the courtesans and everyone else likely to corrupt youth. Queen Henrietta Maria was considered to have been libelled in *Histriomastix* for she was overfond of masques and acted in them. Prynne was sent to the Tower and sentenced by the Star Chamber to life imprisonment after standing in the pillory and having his ears cut off. He continued to write and got himself into more awful trouble by attacking the *Book of Sports* and some of the bishops. This time he had the stumps of his ears cut off and was branded. *

Prynne notwithstanding, the puritans had a hard time of it until the Civil War started. In London, before the theatres were closed, they were opposed by derision and humour. The stage mocked them, getting as many laughs out of their doleful appearance and pronouncements as the twentieth century comic extracts from mothers-in-law. The mockery was distasteful but hardly misdirected. The extreme puritans had little understanding of man's nature and appeared to want to ignore it; by opposing the theatre in general without discrimination and every kind of sport they attempted the impossible to no purpose. And they closed their ears to argument, knowing best direct from God. They would have done well to hearken to Henry Peacham, writing at this time, and well known for his *Compleat Gentleman* (1622).† In a later work *English Recreations* (1641) he wrote: 'For such is our nature, that we cannot stand long bent; but we must have our relaxations as well of mind, as of body.' He suggested suitable recreations for the body including *paille-maille* (or pall mall, a kind of simple croquet with two hoops one at each end of the playing ground, the ball being struck with a mallet) and advised strongly in favour of horse riding from spring to autumn, which

---

*He was by no means finished. He opposed Charles's execution and was imprisoned several more times for disagreeing with the new masters. Ironically, his last position was Keeper of the Records in the Tower of London.

†Henry Peacham (c. 1576–1643), schoolmaster, tutor, author, art collector, musician, painter, mathematician and an expert on heraldry.

gave opportunity to enjoy 'delicate green fields, low meadows, crystal streams, woody hills, parks with deer, hedgerows etc'.

One curious fact about the period of the Civil War and Interregnum was the apparent determination of playwrights to continue writing even if the chances of getting a play performed were small. What with plays, pamphlets and ballads, writing had become an industry and there was an ever growing readership among the recently taught for the printed page. One book, the King James' Bible, appealed to almost everyone and there was hardly an important cleric who did not publish his sermons. The period was notable for its men of learning, many of whom continued their work undismayed by the revolutionary upheavals going on around them. Milton was an exception. He turned to public affairs, reluctantly putting aside his poetical ambitions in favour of pamphleteering: *Of Education* and *Areopagitica* were both published in 1644. Among those undeterred by events were the poet Marvell and Sir William Davenant. The latter was actually encouraged by Cromwell who was satisified with the way Davenant combined plays and masques and in consequence found no difficulty in licensing them. The bulk of the pamphlets and ballads were political and religious, many men being keen to try their hand at influencing others through these media. For readers it was often a kind of entertainment, the ballads particularly because they were fun and promoted laughter.

Music, under puritan surveillance, fared better than the stage. Even Prynne had a kindly word to say about the right kind of music, notwithstanding that organs were being removed from the churches and the masque fast disappearing from the great houses. But there were few of consequence to champion the fiddlers at the inns and taverns; their roguery was obvious and their punishment inevitable. Fortunately Cromwell was musical and unready to be denied the harmless pleasure of listening to players at his receptions as well as in private. He made no fuss about it but he was a valuable patron.

It was a Cromwellian act of political sagacity that exported from Britain's shore some of the most fervent puritans. He stopped monopolies at home and restored monopolies to the private companies that were trading with the Levant, India, the West Indies and America. It was some of these companies, not the government, that made emigration possible for those who wished to found colonies on the east coast of America or for those who sought, for religious reasons, to start afresh. The puritans were by no means the largest number among the emigrants but it happened that they were dominant among those who settled in New England. Their strong feelings about play being sinful because it promoted idleness were there put on trial.

At first, hard relentless work was the only possible recipe for a colony's survival. The English, nevertheless, had brought with them their natural inclination and their memories of pastimes previously enjoyed. They were soon playing bowls, dicing, setting up maypoles and almost equally soon finding that these amusements and all others were banned. They were banned just as resolutely by the churchmen of Virginia as they were by the puritans of the north, the punishments for transgressing the law being comparably severe. The circumstances could dictate no other course. Nevertheless, as time passed the old differences reasserted themselves. When necessity no longer argued that work should fill all the waking hours of day the Virginians countenanced a little amount of play. It was otherwise with the New Englanders. They faced repression of all play, including ornament of dress and smoking, for many more years. Idleness and everything associated with idleness were condemned. *

Ultimately the severity of the puritans' code proved its own undoing. It was established once and for all that men could not live by work alone. Ways round the law were constantly being found. When dancing after weddings was stopped, men and women began attending mid-week lectures with unprecedented enthusiasm for the sake of the opportunities for social intercourse that they gave. Gradually the hold of the puritans grew less firm and by the end of the century events were being held that would have horrified the older generation of immigrants.

It is hard to understand why so many leaders of the colony failed to grasp the necessity of play and the need to channel its direction in preference to attempts at suppression. Their convictions must be accepted without explanation. Here, for example, is William Bradford, the Governor of the Plymouth Plantation, voicing his perplexity: 'Marvellous it may be to see and consider how some kind of wickedness did grow and break forth here, in a land where the same was so much witnessed against and so narrowly looked unto, and severely punished when it was known, as in no place more, or so much, that I have known or heard of; insomuch that they have been somewhat censured even by moderate and good men for severity in punishments. And yet all this could not suppress the breaking out of sundry notorious sins ... especially drunkenness and uncleanness.' Governor Bradford then asked himself to consider whether it was because the Devil worked harder to defeat the churches of Christ or whether it was because wickedness was stopped by strict laws and thus at last broke out wherever it got the chance. His conclusion, gratifying only to the few, was that there was not more evil in the plantation than elsewhere; it only seemed that there was because in the plantation the vigilance was so great that more crimes were detected than elsewhere and made public!

In Connecticut suppressed pastimes included shuffleboard. The Connecticut Law (1650) stated:

Upon complaint of great disorder by the use of the game called shuffleboard, in houses of common entertainment, whereby much precious time is spent unfruitfully, and much waste of wine and beer occasioned; it is therefore ordered and enacted by the authority of this Court, that no person shall henceforth use the said game of shuffleboard in any such house, nor in any other house used as common for such purpose, upon pain for every keeper of such house to forfeit for such offence 20s; and for every person playing at the said game in any such house, to forfeit for every such offence 5s; the like penalty shall be for playing in any place at any unlawful game ...

---

*The inclusion of tobacco was diverting, since the Virginians were already making big profits out of exporting it.

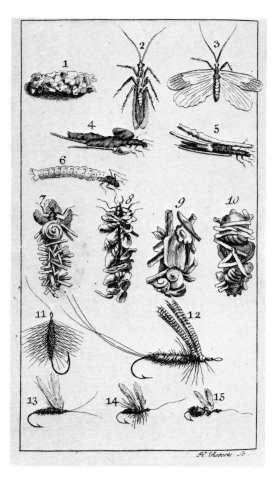

An illustration to an eighteenth century edition of 'The Compleat Angler' showing the real and artificial fly

Nothing, however, was quite as bad in many puritan eyes as 'mixed or promiscuous dancing' and against this practice Increase Mather of New England produced *An Arrow* in 1684. In it he began by affirming such dancing to be utterly unlawful and not to be tolerated. He quoted the Scripture in his support, referred to the unchaste touches and gesticulations and asked, 'who can seriously pray to the Holy God to be with him when he is going to a promiscuous dance?' He was far too late: by the 1680s many members of respectable families in New England were enjoying mixed dancing and, in their opinion, suffering no harm from it. Even at the top there were those who did not show the censorious spirit displayed by Increase Mather. John Winthrop, many times governor of Massachussetts was one; by inclination moderate, he was rebuked on occasions for showing too little zeal in stamping out idleness.

To be fair to the puritans, even in the period of the Interregnum in England they did not everywhere appear as oppressors of innocent pastimes. The words about idleness might thunder from the pulpit but in practice the less deplorable recreations probably carried on much as before. One of these was fishing. A book about it, *The Compleat Angler*, appeared in 1653. * When Isaak Walton wrote it he was living in London and looking back nostalgically to his country boyhood. At the same time he was stating views about recreation that would have been fully acceptable to Mr Peacham and showed no sign that he believed them to be unacceptable to anyone else. Even in the writing of the book he was making 'a recreation of a recreation', and the sub-title of his volume was *The Contemplative Man's Recreation*. Had he been challenged on the value of his book at such a point in history he would have quoted another fisherman of the period, Sir Henry Wootton: 'twas an employment for his idle time, which was then not idly spent'.

So some opportunity for some play there certainly was during the time of the Cromwells; nevertheless by 1653 men were already looking forward to a time when traditional ways would be resumed. But the traditional ways were destined to be spoiled by the unbridled licence of those returning from exile, by the sudden removal of restriction and by an idle court.

---

*Walton was writing just before the invention of the reel, attached first to the thumb and later to the rod. At the same time the needlemakers improved the fishhook.

7

☆ *GENTLEMEN IN TOWN* ☆

Restoration and the Georges

The restoration of the monarchy in the person of Charles II increased the division between courtiers and others, prepared the way for a society dominated by the descriptive phrase 'station in life', and for the rich unfurled a new play called fashion. John Earle, who wrote a book about Bath in 1864, commented that the rise and influence of 'fashion' at this period was unparalleled anywhere in the world. Fashion, he said, was an imitation of court manners, court dress, court talk, court equipages, court eating and drinking, court assembling and dancing and promenading and above all the 'gallantry of coquetting and "courting" '. He added that there had always been a small number of people who imitated the ways of the court, but now that the increase in general wealth had given leisure to a larger group there were many who wanted to be where the fashionable were and where they could be seen themselves—especially the ladies who dragged often unwilling husbands to the spas, Bath being the first among them. For the last word on correct behaviour in this courtly world it is useful to turn to the *Letters* of Lord Chesterfield (1694–1773) to his son on the subject of being well-bred. About play he wrote:

> A gentleman always attends even to the choice of his amusements. If at cards, he will not play at cribbage, all fours, or putt; or in sports of exercise, be seen at skittles, foot-ball, leap-frog, cricket, driving of coaches etc. for he knows that such an imitation of the manners of the mob will indelibly stamp him with vulgarity . . . If you love music, hear it; pay fiddlers to play to you, but never fiddle yourself.

Thanks to the diarists John Evelyn (1620–1706) and Samuel Pepys (1633–1703) information about the Restoration court is more intimate than it might otherwise have been. Pepys, particularly, observed everything and everybody and, more than anything else, he recorded the happenings at the theatre, which demonstrated how cut off more ordinary, God-fearing, though substantial people were to be from the kind of life patronized by Charles and his associates. The fact that the theatre had been restored as the plaything of a tiny minority was to some extent the fault of the Cromwells who had left no theatres to play in. The two new companies were the King's Players and the Duke of York's Men. Both had to wait some years for suitable theatres to be built (the Theatre Royal in Drury Lane for the King's Players) and meantime they performed in small halls in front of small audiences. At first Beaumont and Fletcher were still the favourite dramatists with Shakespeare and Jonson being played occasionally. Because of the frequent

Hard to resist, Nell Gwynne, one of the first actresses and everybody's favourite

change of programme many plays were needed. Davenant, who was in charge of the Duke of York's Men, supplied some of these and Dryden, a newcomer, was a constant contributor. There were also hosts of hack plays which passed muster merely because they gave an opportunity to see a favourite actor or actress in a different part. Thomas Betterton was one of these favourites, 'the best actor in the world'; and among the ladies, apart from favourite Nell Gwynne, were Mrs Bracegirdle and Mrs Oldfield. It was perhaps unfortunate that ladies owed their opportunity for appearing on the stage to Charles II; it hardly gave their reputations, except among the licentious, a fair start. Charles had been familiar during his Paris exile with women playing women's parts. There, however, their names were linked with parts created by some of the greatest dramatists in history, Molière, Racine and Corneille. In England they were associated with mediocrity and lust. 'This night', wrote John Evelyn on 16 January 1662, 'was acted before his Majesty, *The Widow*, a lewd play.'

The susceptible were enchanted; for them the appearance of women on the stage was sensational, almost the most noteworthy event of the Restoration. Pepys could not resist going to the theatre again and again in spite of berating himself constantly for his fondness. 'After dinner . . . my wife [she was not always asked to accompany him] and I to the King's playhouse to see *The Northerne Lasse* . . . Knipp acted it, and did her part very extraordinary well, but the play is but a mean sorry play; but the House very full of gallants . . .' For a while Mrs Knipp (Knepp) was a favourite; Pepys had fondled her in a coach one night after a singing party. Pepys also admired Nell Gwynne, particularly in Dryden's *The Mayden Queene*, which he saw when the King and the Duke of York were present.

If some of the plays were lewd so was the behaviour of the attendant fops, the orange girls and the 'ladies' who joined the audience wearing masks and misbehaving. As for the actresses, they entertained in their dressing rooms, allowing the gallants to loll in carnal luxury while they dressed and undressed. The theatre, in Allardyce Nicoll's phrase, was 'the plaything of society', and that was putting it politely.

Out of this theatrical orgy came a few writers of real merit, the writers of Restoration comedy of whom Congreve was indubitably the best. Their themes were still unpalatable to the many and, to a new audience growing up in the new century, intellectually too sophisticated. Conceivably the theatre might now have recovered a little from its salacious reputation had not Jeremy Collier chosen 1698 for the publication of his polemic *Short View of the Immorality and Profaneness of the English Stage*. 'To sum up the Evidence,' he wrote in his chapter on Immorality Encouraged:

A fine Gentleman is a fine Whoring, Swearing, Smutty, Atheistical Man. These qualities it seems compleat the *Idea* of Honour. They are the Top-Improvements of Fortune, and the distinguishing Glories of Birth and Breeding! This is the *Stage-Test* for *Quality*, and those that can't stand it, ought to be *Disclaim'd*. The Restraints of Conscience and the Pedantry of Virtue, are unbecoming a Cavalier; Future Securities, and Reaching Beyond Life, are Vulgar Provisions: If he falls a Thinking at this rate, he forfeits his Honour: For his Head was only made to run against a Post!

This tiny sample of the style and substance of an attack which ran into nearly 300 pages gives only a trifling indication of the disturbance it caused to a few people. If ignored probably not much attention would have been paid by the public to its strictures, but those attacked could not remain silent, and opportunity was given to Collier to reply and right willingly he did so.

By the time the controversy blew itself out the theatre was left with nothing much. Queen Anne and the Georges did little to encourage drama, and the playwrights who could satisfy the *nouveaux riches* were no better in morals and less talented than their predecessors of the Restoration. A few better plays were in store from Oliver Goldsmith, *She Stoops to Conquer* (1773) and Sheridan's comedies of 1775–9 but meantime even George III complained to Fanny Burney of the lack of good new plays and of the extreme immorality of the old ones. Like others at that time, he was more interested in the players and praised Mrs Siddons, better than Garrick himself, he thought. Garrick was unlucky; he deserved better plays and more discriminating audiences but the more serious men of the day seemed interested only in science. Only in Dublin could the theatre be said to be flourishing.

This situation continued right to the end of this long period. Palatinus, writing in *The Gentleman's Magazine* for August 1816, commented that if only the saloons in the London theatres could be closed and the 'women of the town' prevented from 'obtruding themselves into all parts of the boxes', the morals of the metropolis might be a good deal better. He also advocated 10 pm 'or a little later' as a suitable time for the final nightly curtain, as it was in Edinburgh. By this time, too, even acting was declining in standard: the small intimate theatre, helpful to subtle changes of voice and economy of movement, was giving way to giant auditoriums which encouraged ranting and extravagant gesture. The glory of the stage in the early Victorian era was to be the spectacular.

…ry Lane, the …e of the first …taculars and a … auditorium

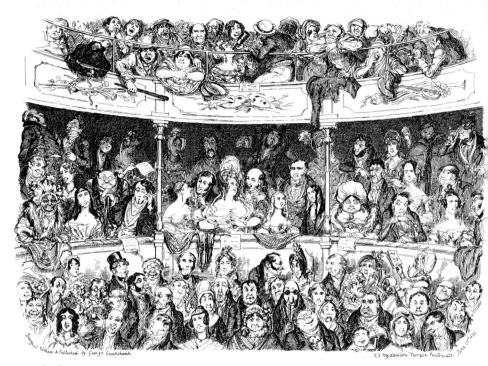

The theatre retained its reputation for rowdy behaviour and licentiousness

However, what the stage could not provide in the late seventeenth and eighteenth centuries, music could. It was the age of the influence of Purcell and Handel; it was the age when music was everywhere, in the gardens, at the spas, at the watering places, in assembly rooms and, most important, in the home. People were not ashamed to take trouble to improve their musical knowledge; Dr Burney, Fanny Burney's father, the musicologist, was a welcome guest in many houses when conversation might turn on the relative merits of songs of other countries. Fanny herself was concerned about a child prodigy who, under tuition, sang three Italian songs 'like a little angel'. She had now given up taking lessons and was singing nothing but French songs! Fanny wished her father could take charge of the girl's training. Pepys, too, was serious about music. He got as far as buying a recorder for himself, 'the sound of it being, of all sounds in the world, most pleasing to me'.

John Evelyn was equally enamoured. 'I dined at Arundel House, where I heard excellent music performed by the ablest masters, both French and English, on theorbos, viols, organs, and voices.' He listened to an Italian playing and singing to the guitar 'with extraordinary skill', and Pepys heard a Frenchman on the same instrument which he thought but a 'bawble' in spite of good playing. The ballad operas gave light music a fresh impetus, Gay's *Beggar's Opera* (how Pepys would have enjoyed it!) and Arne's *Love in a Village* among them. Finally there was Handel to teach Englishmen that grand opera could be enjoyed.

At home, in the salons of the wealthy, people were invited to gather for an evening's elegant entertainment. Some of the best families provided the music themselves and Zoffany's painting of the Granville Sharps shows an attractive if pretentious example of this. Many lower down the social scale were equally happily engaged. Celia Fiennes enjoyed music morning and evening when she was at Tunbridge Wells, and at Devizes, when Mrs Thrale and Fanny Burney were on their way to Bath they were delighted and surprised to hear good pianoforte playing and singing from the daughters of the hostess at The Bear.

Everywhere in the towns of England a small, select society, priding itself on its taste in music, dancing and reading, was being created. The fashionable towns were Bath, Tunbridge Wells, Cheltenham and Harrogate where every provision of elegant play was made for the idle as well as for those who genuinely sought the medicinal value of the water. The spas were fashionable but they had rivals in the seaside towns of Scarborough in the north and Brighton in the south: in the second half of the eighteenth century sea bathing was considered quite as beneficial for health as the baths at the spas (it was even suggested that invalids should drink the water). It was obvious from these developments that one part of society was moving swiftly towards polite, social amusements in which ladies could show their talents at dancing, singing and playing and also engage successfully in conversation with men. And some men were so successful at leaning gracefully over sofas and behaving themselves at balls that it seems hard to fit them into other male activities of the century. It was, however, a charade, played with a great deal of spirit by gentlemen and by small town groups below county level but well above the rest.

London itself was, as usual, the scene of the highest artistic and intellectual attainment and, at the same time, the focal point of the most salacious behaviour. Some of this behaviour went to the spas, watering places and country houses, though modified there by the presence of wives who could not with the same ease be left at home. Viewed from the country the

At the Argyle Rooms where it was fashionable to go if you were fashionable enough to get inside

wickedness of London presented a repellent, Hogarthian picture where the play of 'gentlemen' was almost entirely devoted to disgracing that title. The poet Cowper, not usually forceful, was roused to fury when describing London. He pictured the crowded theatre, the audience with sweating faces outscolding the actors, the placemen waiting in a thoroughly hypocritical, false society. Cowper relied upon his memories, his newspaper reading and his emotions; had he gained access to Boswell's journals his horror would have been ten times worse. Boswell's daily behaviour was certainly deplorable. He saw nothing odd, apparently, in a Sunday spent in church ('I was in an excellent frame and heard service with true devotions'),* partly with a prostitute (worried only because the slut might have deceived him and given him the pox), and partly in gluttonous eating. He was no worse than many others, and better than some for he had occasional twinges of conscience.

In London there were still places where society mixed: men of rank and honour, their wives; gallants, their molls; merchants, their wives; and indeed everyone who could afford to do so either regularly, or on family occasions. These were the gardens: Vauxhall (1661–1859), Ranelagh (1742–1803), Kensington and others. John Evelyn described the New Spring-Garden (Vauxhall) as 'a pretty contrived plantation'; Pepys made many references to it and in one of the last wrote: 'with great pleasure walked, and eat, and drank, and sang, making people come about us to hear us, and two little children of one of our neighbours that happened to be there did come into our arbour, and we made them dance prettily'. On the other hand he found the Mulberry Garden (1668), where Buckingham Palace now stands, 'a very silly place . . . but little company, and those rascally, whoring, roguing sort of people'. A century later Vauxhall was an eighteenth century Disney-land with fireworks and splendid show pieces. Fanny Burney sent her heroine *Evelina* there. She enjoyed the lights and the music and was taken round to see 'various other deceptions'. On the last night of the season, she was informed, there was always a riot and 'such squealing and squalling' as there is on the last night of many events including the twentieth century Proms. At Ranelagh the greatest wonder was the Rotunda, a large circular building, open to the sky when the weather was clement. Concerts were held there and there was a promenade with shops and refreshments. There was also a famous building in the Chinese style.

> Come, come, I am very
> Disposed to be merry—
> So hey! for a wherry
> I beckon and bawl!
> T'is dry, not a damp night,
> And pleasure will tramp light
> To music and lamp-light
> At shining Vauxhall.

The Thames was enjoying its best period at the centre of town as part of

---

*Sermon tasting was an eighteenth century amusement; fashionable preachers drew big crowds.

A Perspective View of the Grand Walk in Vauxhall Gardens and the Orchestra.

Vauxhall Gardens for long a fashionable resort
and a place of elaborate entertainment

Ranelagh. A rival to Vauxhall, the Chinese
House and the Rotunda being exceptionally
admired

The Chinese House, the Rotunda, & the Company in Masquerade
in RANELAGH GARDENS.

La Maison Chinoise la Rotonde et les Masques au Bal Masqué
dans les JARDINS de RANELAGH.

the play scene and the waterman was most profitably employed. Charles Dibdin (1774) wrote about a young and jolly waterman who plied for hire at Blackfriars and so successfully that he was never in want of a fare.

> What sights of fine folks he row'd in his wherry,
> 'Twas clean'd out so nice and so painted withal;
> He was always first oars when the fine city ladies
> In a party to Ranelagh went, or Vauxhall.

Not everyone went to the gardens by boat but many did, and the Thames to country visitors and foreigners was a memorable sight of masts and oars.

The small centre of London was choked with traffic and London entertainment for the fashionable and idle included shopping (with more than average patience required from subservient shopkeepers) and walking in the parks. The opening of St James's Park (1661) fired an encomium of verse from Edmund Waller:

> Of the first Paradise there's nothing found,
> Plants set by Heaven are vanish'd, and the ground:

In 1662 there was skating there and by coincidence Evelyn and Pepys were both there on the same day. Evelyn was impressed by the 'strange and wonderful dexterity' of the sliders performing on skates on the new canal 'after the manner of the Hollanders'. Pepys saw 'people sliding with their skeates, which is a very pretty art' for the first time. He was a bit behind to be seeing it for the first time so he went again a week later and had a fright, for the Duke of York insisted on using his 'scates' 'though the ice was broken and dangerous'. There was no calamity and Pepys commented: 'he slides very well'. 'Skeat' was a Dutch word and skeats were now of iron.

Other eighteenth century meeting places were the coffee houses and the bookshops. The coffee houses were embryo clubs and the recreation there more serious than in the gardens. But it was doing what one liked, men of different interests talking together, often for hours, at little expense to themselves. There the news of the day was exchanged and subjects of mutual concern to the regular patrons discussed. The coffee houses all had names, Lloyd's was among them, and ultimately some became clubs. Meanwhile

> You that delight in wit and mirth,
> And love to hear such news . . .
>
> *　　　*　　　*
>
> Go hear it at a Coffee-house,
> It cannot be but true

Any horseplay that went on in the dark alleys of Vauxhall Gardens and elsewhere was mild in comparison with that of the gangs whose nightly maraudings put ordinary citizens into a state of fear. Most notorious were the Mohocks (derived from the Indian Mohawks) who ran through the streets of London beating people up just for fun, and according to *The Spectator*, 'With razors armed and knives'. Two of their special enjoyments were to roll victims down Snow Hill in tubs, and to overturn coaches on rubbish heaps. These ruffians were not the only ones to misbehave. Gentlemen also indulged

GEO III

Royal Dipping.

Of purest air and healing Waves are full
Where, welcome Maid, Hygeia loves to dwell!
In Holland's Exhibition Rooms may be seen the largest Collection in Europe of Humorous Prints. Admittance One Shilling.

London Pub by Willm Holland, N.º 50 Oxford Str.^t July 15 1789

Bathing in the sea was good for everyone. George III making his first dip in 1789 at Weymouth

Those who had like interests met at their favourite coffee houses to receive and exchange intelligence

...nas ...landson's ...ression of the ...rmen's race ...Doggett's Coat Badge

in evenings of terrorizing. Pictures, drawn by H. Alken in a series of Sporting Anecdotes, from sketches made on the spot, showed these so-called 'sprees' in progress. Dressed in hunting pink the gentlemen are pursuing their spree with the same gusto with which they chased the fox earlier in the day. Under one picture appeared these verses:

> Coming it strong with a Spree and a spread,
> Milling the day-lights or cracking a head;
> Go it ye cripples! come tip us your mauleys,
> Up with the lanterns, and down with the Charleys:
>
> If lagg'd we should get, we can Gammon the Beak,
> Tip the slavies a Billy to stifle their squeak,
> Come the bounce with the snobs, and a —— for their betters
> And prove all the Statutes so many dead letters.

So much for the law; the Beak was quite likely to be related to one of them.

An alternative to rampaging was to indulge in cock-fighting, now organized on a big scale. However enjoyable this continued to be in country areas in pits set up with bales of straw, the pleasure was greater in towns where arrangements could be made for good viewing and for making wagers. At least it made clear, what few doubted at the time, that a good blood-letting was balm for the soul. Often cock-fighting was put on as a sideshow at race meetings. An advertisement for Peterborough Races in 1789, reproduced in

Gentlemen's sprees were all too regular and the terror of law abiding middle class citizens. This one took place at Melton Mowbray

the *Torrington Diaries*, announced: 'There will be a regular Main of Cocks fought at the Angel Inn during the Races, between the Gentlemen of Leicester and the Gentlemen of Peterboro.' Forty years earlier the *Birmingham Gazette* had advertised a Main of Cocks between 'the Gentlemen of Warwickshire and Worcestershire for four guineas a Battle and Forty

Guineas the Main. To weigh on Monday, 9th June and fight the two following days'. Schoolboys in the north were still bringing out their cocks on Shrove Tuesday and showing off their fighting qualities to the gentlemen. In some areas there was an entrance fee, the schoolmaster getting the money, a kind of pre-Easter offering. He also got the dead cocks. Later in the day the cocks refusing to fight were tied to a stake and used as a cock-shy. There was another charge for this. Everywhere it was much the same story. At Lincoln there were cock-pits in the yards of the King's Arms and The Reindeer; Lord Vere Bertie was a patron of the sport and was succeeded later by the Reverend Peregrine Curtois. Lord Monson also participated.

The ability of many men and women to watch pain inflicted on helpless animals and humans has probably not changed; it is the law that has altered. Even so it is hard today to imagine a man of John Evelyn's culture being willing to visit a prison to view a 'malefactor' having 'the question, or torture'. This was in 1651 in Paris, Evelyn giving a detailed description of the body's 'extension' and watching it all. However, when he learned that a second malefactor was to take the place of the first he decided he was 'not able to stay the sight of another'. Hangings continued to be common sport and so thoroughly enjoyed that foreigners continued to comment upon it. Sylas Neville (1767), a minor squire and doctor, told in his diary how he waited for an hour in the lobby of Surgeons Hall to see the body of Mrs Brownrigg, a murderess. It had been brought there after execution to be anatomized. 'A most shocking sight', but one which a great crowd fought to see. Another favourite amusement, like going now to the zoo, was to gape at the lunatics in Bedlam. Boswell went with Dr Johnson in 1775. Boswell was very affected.

Gambling was a compulsion, enjoyed all the more if connected with a contest but enjoyed, often ferociously, in all its many forms. Huge sums were lost at White's and Brooks's, and the sport (or disease) caught men and women of vastly different backgrounds. There was nothing new about gaming; it was as old as mankind, but lately, perhaps because of idleness, it had become an obsession passing out of the realm of play. Horace Walpole was appalled by the grip it had on London and the size of the sums lost and won. Sylas Neville, when still a comparatively poor man in the capital, described a scene at the cock-pit, in these words: 'When one [bird] was killed by the first stroke of his antagonist a great noise is made by the spectators, poulterers, butchers, and other low fellows proposing bets; great anxiety appears on their countenances during the battles. I advised a man, who lost a good deal to stop, but he did not take my advice.' All sports and games were used for betting, even cricket, which was now becoming popular among gentlemen.

Drinking was as fashionable as betting. It was not considered ill-bred to be drunk, and by the middle of the eighteenth century the quantities of spirits, wines and beer consumed were prodigious. Like gaming, the subject is peripheral to play; nevertheless drinking to excess has often been associated with social play and with outdoor games in most centuries—something else foreigners commented upon—but it was only in the eighteenth century that it assumed the mantle of fashion. London at that time was said to have 207

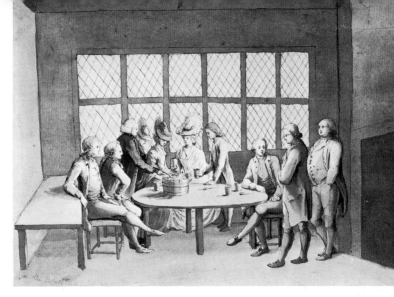

Posset drinking: there were quieter moments and not everyone drank to excess

inns, 447 taverns, 5875 beerhouses and 8659 brandy shops for a population of less than three-quarters of a million.

Dress was another important part of play. According to Mary Moser, in *Nollekens and his Times*, 'Fashion is grown a monster' and Lord Chesterfield wrote to his son in 1748:

> Most of our young fellows here display some character or other by their dress; some affect the tremendous, and wear a great and fiercely cocked hat, an enormous sword, a short waistcoat, and a black cravat . . . others go in brown frocks, leather breeches, great oaken cudgels in their hands, their hats uncocked, and their hair unpowdered . . . A man of sense carefully avoids any particular character in his dress; he is accurately clean for his own sake; but all the rest is for other people's.

Suitably attired, then, the gentleman's chief routine was to appear in idleness at the right places at the right times. Boredom was an enemy only to be defeated when strength of character or strength of inclination caused men to lead individual lives in politics, literature or science. *

The most interesting of the new games, played in a form closely allied to the same sport today, was cricket. It was a phenomenon because it crossed social boundaries and the hero of the day could be a lord's son or his gardener. The Gentlemen of London, like the Gentlemen of other places, took part in matches, but these teams were not composed entirely of gentlemen, since the important—very important because of the betting—consideration was to win. Betting was also responsible for the invention of single-wicket matches between champions sponsored by one gentleman or another. Nevertheless long before the period under review ended, the game had become well established in its own right.†

---

*The Royal Society was founded in 1660.

†The author's copy of Hoyle's *Games Improved* (1779) treats the 'fashionable games', whist, chess, backgammon, draughts etc., also cricket, tennis and billiards. Each section includes 'the method of Betting . . . upon equal or advantageous terms'. Betting is not only on the results of matches but the reasonable odds are given for each stage of a game. The laws of the games are 'as settled and agreed to at White's and Stapleton's Chocolate-houses'.

Cricket had been played in some form by the people at least since the middle of the sixteenth century. It is not difficult to find the occasional reference to it, mostly as an undesirable pastime in puritan times. It picked up immediately in popularity after the Restoration, and some historians have suggested that it was played in private during the Interregnum on the estates of noble lords in England's south-east corner and that this is how it came about that the family and the family servants all appeared together in the same team. At least it was soon clear that lords, enthusiastic gamesters and cricketers, offered jobs to servants who were likely to strengthen the local team. Kent, Hampshire, Sussex and London were the strongholds of cricket and it was the White Conduit Club, playing in the fields of that name in Islington, that brought administrative distinction to the game. Dissatisfied with the ground, but not with the groundsman-bowler, Thomas Lord, the Earl of Winchelsea suggested to him that he should secure a more private field and run it with the financial backing, if need be, of the Earl and Charles Lennox. This Lord did, opening his ground in 1787 and within a year the White Conduit Club had become the Marylebone Cricket Club and, almost immediately, the accepted authority for the game.

Even more surprising than the ease with which cricket established itself as the first major organized sport was the facility it showed in making the laws under which it was to be played. The right of the MCC to revise the rules was never questioned, but the first laws were dated 1744 and were, it would appear, no more than confirmation of earlier ones made at Cambridge about 1700. The laws of 1744 were detailed, beginning 'Ye pitching of ye first Wicket is to be determined by ye cast of a piece of Money'. Hoyle's *Games Improved* (1779) has the laws of cricket as 'revised at the Star and Garter, Pall Mall, February 25, 1774, by a committee of Noblemen and Gentlemen of Kent, Hampshire, Surry [sic], Sussex, Middlesex, and London'. Eleven names are given.

Boxing matches attracted large crowds and boxers were heroes. These two, Humphries and Mendoza, were great rivals

The Hand and Racquet public house is in Whitcomb Street, Westminster, an area where fives and tennis games used to be played

The nobility of the eighteenth century also took a beneficent interest in boxing, though seldom as participants. When fairground fights were restarted victory usually went to the stronger and more vicious contestant. It was the same in the big prize fights. In London there was now some improvements. An early champion, Jack Broughton, succeeded in introducing rules which forbade the wrestling holds and the worst of the in-fighting, putting some premium on skill. He himself lost his title to a tough and rough fighter, Jack Slack, but succeeded nevertheless in starting a boxing school patronized by gentlemen. He included in the training the wearing of coverings for the hands, mufflers, to prevent serious injury, though bare hands were still the custom in actual fights. Soon, at the highest level of the game, skill was succeeding more often than brutality. Two later champions were Daniel Mendoza (1764–1836) and Gentleman Jackson (1769–1845). Both mixed easily with the gentry, some thought absurdly, for the gentlemen appeared to court their company for the sake of reflected glory. Mendoza and Jackson also ran successful schools; Lord Byron was probably one of Gentleman Jackson's pupils. Three thousand people were said to have watched Mendoza fight the 'Gentleman Boxer' Humphries at Stilton in May 1789. Stilton, near Peterborough, was an important stage then on the Great North Road and three thousand not an impossible number. Improvement though there had been, life was still coarse and rough—women were sometimes matched for the fun of seeing them tear at one another—and there was some distance to go before boxing finally accepted the Queensberry rules in 1867.

Tennis was still played. There was a Master of the Royal Tennis Courts in Stuart times and the title was continued even when kings took no interest and general interest in tennis was declining. There were some public courts. The *Hand and Racquet* public house in Whitcomb Street, Piccadilly, is close by a court still discernible in Orange Street and marked with a plaque. Hand and racket indicated that the court was open for games with the racket or without. Probably the great fives player Jack Cavanagh, celebrated in Hazlitt's essay *The Indian Jugglers*, played there. In another place Cavanagh made the meat on the spits tremble on the other side of the wall. There was also billiards, a passion for many men including William Hickey who lists in his Memoirs the tables he frequented as Windmill Street, Whitehall, the Admiralty, the Angel, at the back of St. Clement, and Chancery Lane. Two hours a day was not too long a session for him.

An interesting development of this period was that social reading had become important. Society speculated for weeks about the authorship of *Evelina*. Novelists and poets were not usually in society, but what they wrote, and their presence in town, could be a valuable contribution to society's conversation, the greatest and most prolonged amusement of all. It was an age of tittle-tattle and anything that enabled a man or a woman to contribute a new piece of intelligence or gossip to the common pool was welcomed. It helped the day along. So books were read and talked about, and books were bought, and borrowed from the new circulating libraries in London and the provinces, particularly in the fashionable resorts. These libraries were a boon and owed their existence to the advent of the novel.

One town that came into its own during the Napoleonic wars was Edinburgh. For long a most important centre of literature and learning it had lacked the attraction necessary to draw Englishmen north. Now they came and helped to approve an elegant style that Edinburgh was not to lose until, like everywhere else, elegance was submerged by the demands and needs of the common man.

By the end of the eighteenth century there were many public billiard rooms

8

☆ GENTLEMEN IN THE COUNTRY ☆

Restoration and the Georges

The countryside was also changing, not perhaps obviously to the eye but radically. The smaller squires were selling out to the bigger landlords; the bigger landlords, much to the dismay of Lord Torrington as he confided in his diaries, were often absent in London, leaving the management of their estates to servants. The forest laws, which were not quite forgotten in 1660, were being replaced by the game laws and for the country the era of the gamekeeper had begun.

> To all People whom these Presents may concern: Know ye, that I, R.P. of etc. Esq., Lord of the Manor of G. in the County of H. do hereby make, constitute and appoint W.W. of, etc., who is truly and properly my servant, to be my Game-keeper within my said Manor, according to an Act of Parliament in that case made, in the third year of the Reign of King George the First, during my Will and Pleasure; and I do also hereby authorize the said W.W. by Virtue of another Act of Parliament in that Case made, to take away any Hare, Pheasant, Partridge, or any other Game, which he shall find in the Custody of any Person or Persons within my said Manor, not being duly qualified to kill the Game; and also to seize and take away, for my Use, all grey-hounds, setting-dogs, lurchers, or other Dogs, to kill Hares or Conies; Guns, Nets or other instruments for the Destruction of the Game, from any Person or Persons within my said Manor, not being duly qualified to use the same etc. *

So, in this respect the years made no difference. The birds and beasts of the fields and woods and the fishes in the lakes and streams were still the property of those who owned the land. They were imperative for the gentleman's play, a more important factor than the people's needs. For the gentleman at the beginning of the eighteenth century the hare was still the favourite quarry. A compendium of the countryside *Dictionarium Rusticum et Urbanicum*, 1704 (mercifully with only the title in Latin) commented; 'of all the Chases the Hare makes the greatest Pastime and Pleasure for 'tis great satisfaction to see the craft used by this little Animal'. The elaborate ritual of fox hunting had not been evolved; it was still a matter of debate whether it was better to hunt with hounds or course with greyhounds.

Sportsmanship was unencumbered with fanciful notions of fair play. Men were busy most of the time with nets and other engines of destruction, the object being to entice or terrify birds and small animals into them. It was a matter of choice whether a bird was shot when on the ground or in the air; it

---

*The Laws of England Concerning the Game. Third edition with additions, 1736.

depended on how keen the sportsman was to show his skill in preference to counting his bag. The *Dictionarium Rusticum* was full of illustrations of nets. Bramble-nets were for catching small birds, a clap-net was for larks, draw-nets were for larger birds. On a moonless night for preference, a gentleman could enjoy bat-fowling, achieved by lighting straw and beating the nearby hedges so that the roosting birds awoke and made for the flames. Various nets could be made for catching fish, making the art of Isaak Walton look almost dilettante. One entry in the dictionary had a modern ring:

> PADDOCK-COURSE. Paddock is a piece of Ground encompassed with Pales, or a Wall, and most conveniently taken out of a Park; it must be a Mile long, and about a quarter of a Mile broad; but the further end should be somewhat broader than the nearer, and that because most people desire to see the end of the Course, and who wins the Wager. At the hither end must be the Dogs-house, where the Dogs are kept that are to Run the Course, which must be attended by two Men, and one of them is to stand at the Door to slip the Dogs, but the other must be a little without the Door, to slip the Teazer, to drive away the Deer. On the other side must be made three Pens, for as many Deer as is designed for the Course; and there must be also a Keeper or two, to turn the Deer out for the Course which Deer are to run all along by the Pale, and, on the other side, at the same distance, stand the spectators. There are Posts along the Course. The low Post is 160 yards distant from the Dog-house and Pens and when the Deer reach it the Dogs are released. There follow the $\frac{1}{4}$ mile post, the $\frac{1}{2}$ mile post, the pinching post and then the ditch where the deer get away from the dogs. First dog to leap the ditch wins.

The *Dictionary* and the *Laws of England Concerning Game* establish how general fields sports had become and how romanticized. John Gay wrote a long poem, *Rural Sports* (1713), on the theme. It was amusingly extravagant in places, beginning with the poet's misfortune to be immured in the noisie town, respiring its smoke, and going on to describe the delights of fishing, hare hunting, fowling, and riding the horse in the chase after stag and fox. Again the acceptance of the pain inflicted on the hunted, which was part of the pleasure, is included with love of the countryside and devotion to horses and dogs. Even the gentle Cowper accepted these conventions. He, too, loved the chase and described with gusto the harmless pursuit after one of his pet hares. More surprisingly he counted himself fortunate to be present when a fox was caught by dogs in the Throckmortons' park. Gay wrote of a good catch:

> Now, happy fisherman, now twitch the line!
> How thy rod bends! behold, the prize is thine!
> Cast on the bank, he dies with gasping pains,
> And trickling blood his silver mail distains.

Lord Torrington (John Byng) made a good defence, in eighteenth century terms, of cruelty in the chase. The Byng family were staying at Biggleswade, a favourite area for them. He was up betimes with his sons to go ferreting. 'Mamma', he wrote, 'thinks us cruel; but from our cradle there is love of field sports handed down to us from Nimrod; and confirmed by the Norman

(above left) *The gentlemen of the country*
[inc]luded fowling which meant shooting birds by
[mo]re than one method

(above right) Birds were also killed by hawks
[wh]ose skill was much admired

Birds were also netted: there were nets of
ingenious kinds

Conquest; as *a right of gentry* [author's italics]: Nor do I hope to live to see the Sans Culottes* of this land laying all distinction waste . . .' Torrington put his views into practice by hunting the hare as often as possible on Royston Heath when he was staying at Baldock.†

By this date (1794) Torrington was in a minority, for the gentry had lost much of their interest in the hare and had turned their attention to the fox. Part of the reason for this lay in the pleasure of sitting astride a horse, the social arrangements for the meet and the dressing up which was becoming fashionable in the best hunts. The Reverend Benjamin Newton, Rector of Wath, Yorkshire, put this point nicely in an entry in his diary: 'I go shooting for health and hunting for society which I like to meet better in the field than at any dinner where I must drink more than I like.' And in another entry he remarked: 'Went hunting with Mr. Bell's hounds, had tolerable sport, these hounds please me much as they are attended by gentlemen only, no farmers.' Newton did his job well but, as a gentleman, he liked to be among gentleman and on the right kind of horse. The point was commonly accepted. It was said of Mr Hugo Meynell, Master of the Quorn for nearly fifty years at the end of the eighteenth century, that he could not have been so successful 'had not his conduct from the commencement to the close of his career been characterized by the deportment which distinguished a thoroughbred English gentleman'. There were other kinds of fox hunters and not all of them farmers. 'Tear him and eat him!' was the cry as 'down went the fox, crash into' the mouths of the hounds, as related by Mr Surtees in *Handley Cross*. All the same, the foxhunter in his scarlet or black coat immaculately turned out on his shining, groomed horse, attending the meet outside *The Fox and Hounds*, was to be for at least 150 years an almanack view of gentlemanly perfection. He was, with his lady, the patrician of the countryside, asking no more from those on foot than that they should open the gate, to be rewarded at best with a smile, or at worst with a flick of the whip.

The scene was not unlike that at the races. Here were paddocks for the gentry and the rails for the rest. The races were a common pleasure and each side was aware of the other and even conversed, provided the first principles of 'station in life' were observed. Most diaries and letters of the period mention the races. Evelyn went to Newmarket where the King had a house. He visited the stables and saw where the horses were kept at 'vast expense' and 'with all the art and tenderness imaginable', and on the heath he saw a match between horses owned by the King and a Mr Eliot. Thousands turned out to see it. Pepys referred to horse racing but appeared unmoved; Defoe described the races in his *Tour Through England and Wales*; Celia Fiennes was at Epsom races where there were rooms for gaming. The first Bedford Races were held in Cow Meadow in 1730, the promoters being the third Duke of Bedford and Sir Humphrey Monoux. Sylas Neville in 1771 described those

---

Sans-culottes was the name given by aristocrats of France during the Revolution to the extremists of the working classes. Fresh in Torrington's mind of course, for this was 1794.

† Mrs Byng was not alone in thinking hunting cruel. William Cobbett was well aware of the need to defend his passion for hare hunting, one of the defences being that it was 'inseparable from early rising'.

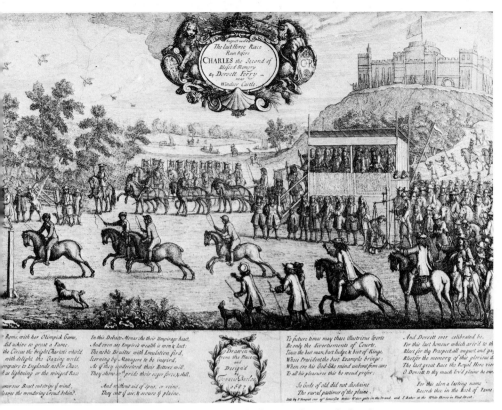

Charles II was an enthusiast for racing. This was the last race he watched and presumably he is in the grandstand. Note the scales

involved at Newmarket as a strange collection of lords, lackeys, jockeys and blacklegs (ie swindlers); he appeared to disapprove but went to races fairly often nonetheless. Torrington was not a great race-goer but he was a connoisseur of courses, mentioning Bedford, Worcester, Hereford, Llandaff, Cowbridge, Lewes, Chesterfield, Derby, Knutsford ('not large enough for a goose to run round'), Stamford, Peterborough, York and Faversham. Lincoln was well known but not so good (socially) as Nottingham. Southwold tried races on the common in 1820. Newton enjoyed himself when he visited Catterick, seeing good sport and 'all the principal people of the neighbourhood'. He went to Richmond races (also in Yorkshire). Everywhere there was usually 'a great concourse' of people.

It was the enthusiasm of Charles II that established Newmarket as the headquarters of racing and breeding horses; here matches for money and plate races for trophies attracted thousands of spectators. The smaller race courses seldom staged important matches and prizes were often saddle, bridle and whip. Ascot followed Newmarket in importance in Queen Anne's reign and Epsom's comparative obscurity came to an end with the first Derby in 1780. All the classic races made a beginning in this period, the Racing Calendar was first published in 1727; the Jockey Club, the controlling body, was founded in 1750, and the Stud Book first published before the century's end. The importance of these developments for racing was very great and at the same time a precedent was set for the proper control and organization of other sports.

Races between men were also popular in the eighteenth century, when champions would be matched by their backers in the same way as horses. Celia Fiennes referred to a race of 22 miles round a 4 mile course at Windsor between two footmen, English and Scottish. It was a good race, with the Scotsman beating the Englishman after the Englishman had led most of the way. Celia Fiennes applauded the Scotsman for saving himself for the 'last push'. The race took two and a half hours. Sometimes races between men, boys or even women took place at horserace meetings, fairs or village feasts, as diversions. Making a match and betting on it was the real excitement.

The phenomenon of the eighteenth century was the rise of cricket as a truly popular game. Its organization at the top was dealt with in the previous chapter, but in the countryside it was equally enjoyed and everywhere talked about. By 1740, judging by the illustrations, dress was not unimportant: the players are all wearing caps and knee breeches (when trousers were introduced there was objection to them because they were thought to get in the way). The illustration also shows that there is no middle stump: the wicket with its bail still resembles the narrow hurdle entrance to a sheep pen, also called a wicket, and believed by some to be the origin of the one for cricket. The bat is curved and heavy, to deal with the ball bowled underhand and fast along the ground (as in bowling, as the name implies). Round-arm bowling was not introduced until the beginning of the nineteenth century, and was regarded, rightly, as a revolution. The umpires also have bats, perhaps to protect themselves or because at some time in the evolution of the game a run was not completed unless the umpire's bat was touched. The couple sitting in the field of play are the scorers, doing their duty by notching runs on a stick.

An early cricket match. Note the scorers, notching the runs on the field of play

Cricket had an additional advantage over other games: it was pleasing to the eye and for this reason could be enjoyed by women who had little other interest in the match; it also had style and was therefore fashionable. The fourth Duke of Bedford encouraged the game in Woburn Park; the Duke and Duchess of Ancaster were among the distinguished spectators who watched a match between six professionals and five gentlemen for Hampshire against a similarly selected team for England. Sylas Neville, after dining in Yarmouth, went with his host and other gentlemen to see a cricket match. 'It is too violent an exercise for me, otherwise I should like it.' A few eyebrows were raised at the close association on the field of play of gentlemen and professional players, but the fascination of the game (and the money involved in winning) triumphed over social misgivings. Perhaps it was now that the phrase 'one of nature's gentlemen' was first used. Gentlemen were always pleased if they could hand out this accolade to their professional friends and quite a number deserved it. The game had other critics. Horace Walpole was one. 'He is gone to a cricket match, from which your letter has saved me.' And there was worse. In 1749: 'I could tell you of Lord Mountford's making cricket matches, and fetching up parsons by express from different parts of England to play matches on Richmond Green.' That was a danger one distinguished player foresaw. Henry Venn of Huddersfield and Cambridge University, after a good innings in a match between Surrey and All England, flung down his bat with the memorable words: 'I will never have it said of me, "Well struck parson!" ' He retired from the game: he was to be ordained the following week.

Other parsons were not so fussy, though no doubt they also were doing a good job in their parishes. Crabbe's parson in 'The Village' (1783) was

A sportsman keen, he shoots through half the day,
And, skill'd at whist, devotes the night to play . . .

The main delight of Parson Woodforde in Norfolk in the late 1700s was the theatre, and he did his best to travel to Norwich whenever possible to see a show. He never failed to comment on the performances: 'The play was Hamlet and the Entertainment, The Camp. The play was very well but the other like a puppet show, fit only for children.' This form of entertainment, a serious play followed by a farce or light comedy, remained a feature of provincial life for many years and was still being used in parts of Ireland until quite recently.

Among field sports, fishing and coursing hares were Parson Woodforde's chief recreations: 'my young Greyhound, Hector, performed incomparably'. On the whole, however, he seems to have been neither below gentlemen's pursuits nor above those which interested the villagers. Most games of the times were mentioned in the diary which covered the very long period of 1758–1803. When young he went bear-baiting and cock-fighting; he played draughts and battledore and shuttlecock ('kept the cock up once upwards 500 times'); he had a fives court in his churchyard; he played card games of several kinds and danced. He was very fond of food and drink, and hospitable: 'My Frolic for my people to pay Tithe to me this day. I gave them a good dinner . . . they drank of wine 6 Bottles, of Rum 1 gallon and half, and I know not what ale.'

Woodforde had a much warmer interest in the poor than the Reverend Newton and he will be heard of again in another chapter. Newton did everything a gentlemen was supposed to do, including his duty, but does not seem to have gone beyond that, at least in the short period that his diary covers, 1816–18. He played chess ('with Mr. Assey who beat me very much, I attribute it to playing with the red men instead of the white to which I am most accustomed'); he mentioned cricket but did not play; he danced 'with great glee'; he hunted often; coursed often ('went coursing to Norton with Mr. Morely where at least 200 people were assembled and 8 brace of hares killed'); he went to races, visited big houses like any modern tourist, dined out often, played whist and backgammon and had the right thoughts about poaching: 'Went on Justice business to Col. Serjeantson's, convicted George Fletcher in £5 penalty for snigling' (ie catching eels with baited hooks). He shot and although not so keen on his food as Woodforde referred to it often enough: 'The most remarkable occurrence was Walker's eating, 1st. a plate of haddock, 2nd. a plate of fillet of veal and being twice helped to tongue, 3rd. three slices of a saddle of mutton, 4th. a large wing of a large duck, 5th. two plates of roasting pig, 6th. half the tail of a large lobster, 7th. cheese and then dessert. N.B. He had no wager on his eating.' Newton's daughters went sea-bathing and he, himself, at Boro'bridge Fair, saw Polito's wild beasts. He also went with a party to the Circus of Horsemanship 'to the benefit of Miss Bannister, a famous equestrian heroine'. He was so impressed with the performance that he allowed a party of servants, including his own, to go on another day from Wath and Melmerby. Newton's rectory at Wath can still be admired from a bend in the road, a lovely place.

Across the Atlantic recreational life on the eastern seaboard of America was a modification, with one big exception, of that in England. Puritan restraint

Thomas Bewick's reputation for illustrating country ways is second to none. A man fishing in the river and two sportsmen on the seashore are among the well known examples of his art

was losing its power; divisions between society were increasing but rich and poor alike were growing more and more pleasure loving. Officially apprentices were still prevented from enjoying themselves at cards, dice or other unlawful games, and puritans still howled their threats at members of the more fashionable society who went to plays, dances and card parties. But the big exception to any comparison with England was that the land teamed with game of many kinds and there was plenty of meat for all. There were bears, buffaloes, panther, deer, beavers, otters, foxes, raccoons, hares, wild cats, musk rats, squirrels, opossums, eagles, turkeys, cranes, herons and dozens more of different kinds of birds and fish. Plenty, in fact, to hunt and plenty to eat. There was still hard work to be done but everyone knew that relaxation would follow at fairs, corn-huskings and barn-raisings. Making music and dancing were very popular and, as in medieval England (except that the weapons were no longer the same), target shooting was encouraged, for life depended on the ability to shoot and to shoot well.

Foster Rhea Dulles in *America Learns to Play* (1940) quoted examples of wild enjoyment at husking-bees ('neighborly gatherings of farm families to husk corn', according to Webster's Dictionary) which shocked the older generation and led to appearances in court. Bull- and bear-baiting were among American sports; so were cock-fights and football. Cruelty and brutality were international. On more tranquil occasions cricket and bowls were enjoyed and in winter, ice sports. Horse racing was a passion. Like the inns in England, the American taverns played their part, arranging cock-fights and putting up cocks for marks. All English and Dutch sports of the eighteenth century, down to tennis and fives, were recorded: the climate and the environment promoted the popularity of one sport and lessened that of another but basically it was the mixture as in England with no sign that a sickening journey of 3000 miles had in any way abated man's fondness for play.

In New York, Boston and Philadelphia the new aristocracy were dressing up and enjoying themselves with undreamed of ostentation and elegance. Dancing, theatre-going, concerts and sleighing parties were among the pleasures, always to the accompaniment of eating and drinking. This behaviour did not please everybody. There were moves to curtail their enjoyments and Thomas Jefferson, after the American Revolution, taking a more serious view of life, tried to break cultural as well as political ties with England. Somewhat unfairly he argued against sending young Americans to Europe to finish their education for 'if he goes to England he learns drinking, horse racing and boxing'. For a time the Revolution reduced frivolity, but once the new century was safely launched Americans renewed their play with enviable vigour.

9

☆ *THE POOR* ☆

Restoration and the Georges

Life for the poor has seldom been easy, but there have been times in history when, through one agency or another, something has been done to alleviate their lot, whereas at other times the whole weight of the rest of society has seemed bent on crushing them. This was one of the bad periods. In the country the selfishness of landlords over the game laws and their absenteeism leading to impersonal control were preliminary to a second round of enclosures and the loss of more common land. Many of the poor left the countryside to join the factory workers in the mills, but the towns had made no provision for their happiness, only for their labour, and soon the workers were either too weak or too weary to play. One curious fact is that John Wesley's Methodist Movement, which flourished so readily among the poor during the second half of the eighteenth century and the early part of the nineteenth, did little to moderate the misery of being poor. In some ways it increased it. There was no room for play in the Methodist gospel and it saw nothing particularly wrong in disciplining small children for work in the factories with no recreational time off, or strength to indulge in play if time were allotted. Socially the Methodists were another sect of puritans denying the evidence before their own eyes that play was necessary to men, women and children. But Methodism brought its own consolations. It was an emotional religion and members were expected to demonstrate their feelings. They did so in their religious services, thus gaining relief from frustrations in the same way that games players were discharged of theirs. They also gained a sense of purpose.

As the law stood in 1666, the countryman who was not privileged in some way had few rights of play and a great many perils to avoid. Much depended, therefore, on how easily or harshly the law was administered. *The Complete Justice: A Compendium of the particulars incident to Justices of the Peace (1638)* enshrined the power of the gentry. 'Unlawful games' could be interpreted as a justice (a landowner) willed, for he had power to enter any 'common place' where there was any 'playing at dice, tables, cards, bowles, coits, tennis, casting the stone, football or other unlawful game now invented, and hereafter to be invented', and to arrest the keeper of such a place and imprison him until he found 'sureties by recognizance no longer to use such house, game, play, alley or place'. He could also imprison the players, but who was liable to arrest? Not gentlemen, unless they happened to be students, as the next paragraph spelt out:

Artificer of any occupation, or any husbandman, apprentice, labourer, servant at husbandry, journeyman, servant of artificer, mariner, fisherman, waterman, or servingman, other than of a Nobleman or of him that may dispend 100 pounds by the yeare, playing within the precinct of his master's house, shall not play out of Christmas at any unlawful game, or in Christmas out of the house or presence of his master.

The fine was 8d for each offence. Other games were mentioned without making it clear that they were necessarily unlawful. These were 'the morrice and other open dances, bear-baitings, and common-playes'. For further information the compiler referred the reader to the entry, SUNDAY.

The SUNDAY entry, after rehearsing the penalties for non-attendance at church, continued: 'There shall be no meeting, assemblies or concourse of people for any sports or pastimes out of their own parishes on the Lord's day; nor bear-baiting, bull baiting, interludes, common playes, or other unlawful exercises within their own parishes.' If unable to pay the fine the offender was to be put in the stocks for three hours; maybe, particularly after the Restoration, the risk was well worth taking. Not that it would appear that there was much opportunity for enjoying play outside the parish since church had to be attended first and there was no transport available for getting to another place. On Sunday no 'carryers, waggoners, waynmen, drovers' were allowed to drive their carts or their animals.* However, in spite of the difficulties, gangs from elsewhere did break up play on occasions.

The protection of the gentry's rights to the birds, beasts and fishes of the fields, woods and streams was in theory total, and enforcement probably much more to the magistrate's liking. 'One Justice of Peace, upon information of any unlawful hunting of Deere or Conyes by night, or with painted faces, or other disguising in forest, park or warren' could 'make warrant to the Sherriffe' and woe to the man who concealed the hunting or the name of any companion. Hunting by three or more was considered a riot. The penalty for those entering any enclosed ground reserved for deer or conies and chasing and killing them was three months' imprisonment without bail and to continue in prison until treble damages and costs were paid. Much the same penalty was demanded from anyone keeping a greyhound to course deer or hares, unless the offender had lands to be inherited of certain value, goods of certain value or was the son 'of a Knight or Baron of parliament, or son and heir of an Esquire'. Further, any man having land worth £100 and finding there another with land of £40 or less with a gun, bow, dogs, or engines for killing deer or hares could take them from him and make use of them. Taking of hawk's eggs was also an offence punishable with three months in prison and the necessity of finding sureties for the culprit's good behaviour for seven years. That must surely have been difficult on occasions. Pheasants, partridges, pigeons, herons, mallard, duck, teal, widgeon, grouse, heathcock, or moor-game were also protected from anyone without the right gentlemanly qualifications. Gilbert White's view expressed in his *Natural History of Selborne* (1789) is revealing:

Though large herds of deer do much harm to the neighbourhood, yet the injury to

---

*The salesman also got a warning: 'Shewing of boots on the Sunday, with intent to sell them, loseth 3 shillings 4 pence, and the value of the boots.'

the morals of the people is of more moment than the loss of their crops. The temptation is irresistible; for most men are sportsmen by constitution: and there is such an inherent spirit for hunting in human nature, as scarce any inhibitions can restrain. Hence, towards the beginning of this century all this country was wild about deer-stealing. Unless he was a hunter, as they affected to call themselves, no young person was allowed to be possessed of manhood or gallantry.

Grim as this law was for the poor in many areas, in others they probably got along quite reasonably if the organization for apprehending malefactors was slack, or the local squire an easy-going despot who regarded sporting instincts as natural if they did not go too far. In mountainous Caernarvon, for example, according to the author of *Recreations in Natural History* (1815) fox hunting was pursued on foot and was enjoyed in consequence by the 'commonalty'. Their only need was a 'leaping pole' to negotiate the stream and bogs. But sturdy independence, highly praised in the days of the long-bow, became less and less a virtue as the years rolled on and society at the top and bottom drifted further and further apart. By the end of the period the poor were being derided for being poor and—whether or not existence was as bad as described by J. L. and Barbara Hammond in *The Village Labourer 1760–1832*—the legal facts and the debates in Parliament showed con-clusively that life for many under the Game Laws was even more fearful than it had been under the Forest Charter of medieval times. Several new acts were responsible for this, each one of which increased the penalties for poaching until transportation for seven years and the use of spring guns and man-traps stirred enough people to protest. Until then it had begun to appear that there were no limits to which gentlemen would not go to protect their play. 'The rulers who ride the people', wrote Sydney Smith in the *Edinburgh Review* (1821), 'never think of coaxing and patting till they have worn out the lashes of their whips and broken the rowels of their spurs.'

William Cobbett, ignoring temporarily the game laws, wrote with customary hyperbole of the happiness and delights of the poor a century before the publication of his *Rural Rides* (1816). Certainly it was possible to paint a pretty picture of the traditional village wakes or feasts, held at the time of year when farming needs were small. Wakes and feasts often went on for several days and were used to commemorate the anniversary of the dedication of the parish church. In many places there would be more than one feast in the year and sometimes as many as three. Parishes without a wake or feast of their own often joined forces with a neighbour. Week-long wakes were not unknown and, when thoroughly secularized, particularly in growing urban areas, turned themselves into holiday weeks when factories would close down. In addition, there was a medley of pagan, Christian and political holidays associated with May Day, Christmas, Guy Fawkes, Plough Monday, Shrove Tuesday and, in some villages where a Tory squire ruled, Oak Apple Day to celebrate Charles II's birthday and his miraculous escape from the Roundheads when hiding in an oak-tree. All these days were opportunities for play, including eating and drinking and every kind of harmless entertainment ranging from foot races and trials of strength and skill to trying to catch a greased pig and making the funniest face through a horse collar—all amusements that more recently have been associated with

The Olney pancake race of today probably causes less laughter and excitement than the earlier shift races for women at village fairs

village and church fêtes.

These wakes, feasts and special holidays were not the only breaks to a routine of Sunday and a six-day working week. Depending on where a man lived, there were opportunities for play at the trade fairs, when showmen and travelling performers drew the crowds which were ever ready to be entertained, scared, and amazed while the more serious business of stocking up with goods and equipment went on. Hiring-fairs also, on a less elaborate scale, gave the young a further chance for enjoyment. Much of the fun was only slap-and-tickle, though an examination of the sideshows would reveal how versatile the showmen were in providing outlets for every need and taste. Practically everybody went. Sylas Neville confided to his diary: 'was persuaded to go to Gorlston Fair, much frequented by the low people, particularly the more profligate'. Soon he was writing again: 'My people being gone to Ingham Fair, shall be alone till tomorrow evening'. Fortunately 'the low people' could not be kept out and, generally, it was they who added to the fun by being more ready than their betters to 'walk up' and try their skill, or to show their courage by lasting a minute with a prize-fighter in the ring. Not everyone lived near enough to a fair to be able to attend without permission for time off from their masters. By tradition it was usually granted, and a day spent in this way was looked forward to for weeks.

It was still Sunday, however, that provided the regular play, and the number of games enjoyed on that day makes a surprisingly long list. Besides football, cricket, wrestling and cock-fighting there were cudgel-playing and single stick (cudgel-players had two clubs), bowling and bell-ringing, running at the quintain, quoits, fives, foot-races, stool-ball and skittles (Torrington watched Dutch prisoners playing it). Woodforde recorded all fours, a card game, but not on Sunday, and on special occasions there was a women's race for a smock or shift which usually drew a crowd. Torrington also described what he called a county game, the Cheshire militia playing prisoners' bars, 'a sport of mere agility and seemingly productive of quarrels'.* Many children's games were continued into manhood, particularly leap-frog and others which involved leaping and dashing about.

It was obviously better when all these games were being played with the squire and farmers present, than later when absentee landlords were commonplace and Cobbett could write: 'I repeat, that the baseness of the English land-owners surpasses that of any other men that ever lived in the world. The cowards know well that the labourers that give value to their land are skin and bone.' All the same, and in spite of the widening gap between countryman and gentry, there was conflict of evidence and not everyone looked back nostalgically. Another who did was Robert Bloomfield. He confirmed the social distinctions in the earlier society but recalled the happiness of the Harvest Home, now (1798) fast disappearing:

> Behold the sound oak table's massy frame
> Bestride the kitchen floor! the careful dame
> And gen'rous host invite their friends around
> While all that clear'd the crop, or till'd the ground
> Are guests by right of custom: old and young,
> And many a neighbouring yeoman, join the throng,
> With artizans that lent their dext'rous aid,
> When o'er each field the flaming sunbeams play'd . . .

And when the eating was done

> And crackling music, with the frequent song,
> Unheeded bear the midnight hour along.
> Here once a year distinction lowers its crest.—
> The master, servant, and the merry guest,
> Are equal all; and round the happy ring
> The reaper's eyes exulting glances fling.

Miss Mitford, writing about Berkshire (1819), saw it differently; through her eyes the present was still good: 'As party produces party, and festival brings forth festival, in higher life, so one scene of rural festivity is pretty sure to be followed by another. The boys' cricket match at Whitsuntide . . . patronised by the young lord of the manor and several of the gentry round, and followed by jumping in sacks, riding donkey races, grinning through horse-collars, and other diversions . . .' was followed by 'a Maying in full form in Whitley-wood' at the beginning of July ('What's in a name?' asks Miss Mitford), between hay-time and harvest. The festival was helped by the presence of gentlemen headed by 'that very genial person, our young lord of the manor' but it was organized by 'mine host of the Rose' with his 'well

---

*Strutt, with no opportunity to read the Torrington diaries, wrote ten years later about prisoners' bars: 'the success of this pastime depends upon the agility of the candidates and their skill in running, especially in Cheshire'.

known diligence, zeal, activity, and intelligence'. 'How could a Maying fail under such auspices?'

How indeed, for the country was beginning to depend even more than previously on the innkeeper whose opportunity this was to replace the absentee squire as patron of village activities. The opportunity was all the greater since the parson was so often a gentleman whose interests were the same as the squire's and his absences sometimes as regular. So it was the innkeeper who distributed small patronages, kept the bowling green, arranged wagers for contests between cocks and between men, and welcomed the gentry when they met for sport. Many parsons were out with the gun or the hounds, and in the evening, after heavy dining and wining would join the decorative, inactive (apart from playing the piano), devitalized (to borrow Professor G. M. Trevelyan's word) women in the drawing room. No wonder these ladies maddened John Wesley, Hannah More and others who rightly resented women's willingness to suppress their physical vigour in favour of a new convention of female helplessness.

The ladies, nevertheless, seemed always to travel with their husbands and to suffer, if necessary, the rigours of nights at the inns. On many of these occasions their husbands were there for the sport, hunting the fox or hare, shooting or fishing. Everywhere the inn signs reflected these activities: The Anglers' Rest, The Fighting Cocks, The Fox and Hounds, The Bear, The Cricketers and some less hackneyed like The Dog and Partridge. Some were good, some were bad and Torrington who travelled a great deal seldom failed to comment. 'The Hop Pole at Ollerton is pleasantly situated upon a trout stream, and fronting the forest woods; a house of good stop, and station. Here we fared comfortably.' The innkeeper, no doubt, was helped in some villages by the schoolmaster or shopkeeper, somebody a little above the average in ability but more controlled than Thomas Turner of East Hoathly whose struggles to keep sober were often unrewarded. 'After supper our behaviour was far from that of serious, harmless mirth, it was downright obstreperious . . . Our diversion was dancing, or jumping about, without a violin or any musick, singing of foolish healths, and drinking all the time as fast as it could well be poured down.'

The inn could be a comfortable place for the poor in winter when part of the inkeeper's welcome was to keep everybody warm. In summer, too, it was pleasant to sit outside, gossiping, watching the world go by and perhaps some sport on the green. There, too, it was possible to wait for the coach to arrive with its news, and perhaps passengers, to make talking points for succeeding days.

> Hark! t'is the twanging horn o'er yonder bridge,
> That with its wearisome but needful length
> Bestrides the wintry flood, in which the moon
> Sees her unwrinkled face reflected bright:-
> He comes, the herald of a noisy world,
> With spatter'd boots, strapp'd waist, and frozen locks;
> News from all nations lumb'ring at his back.
> . . . his one concern
> Is to conduct it to the destined inn: Cowper 'The Task' (1785)

The village inn was a meeting place for everyone and a good innkeeper was an important organizer of sport and merriment

But it was summer when the farmer's boy, getting the pleasure that comes as readily to poor as to the rich, looked upon a maid and started another chapter of that endless play of life.

> There half revealing to the eager sight
> Her full-ripe bosom, exquisitely white.
> In many a local tale of harmless mirth,
> And many a joke of momentary birth,
> She bears a part, and as she stops to speak,
> Strokes back the ringlets from her glowing cheeks.
>
> Bloomfield. 'The Farmer's Boy' (1800)

Had he lived in East Anglia the farmer's boy might well in winter have taken part in a game of football called in those parts, camping. It was a wild ferocious game, much dreaded by sober citizens and employers; much looked forward to by expectant players and spectators. Joseph Pennell recalls tales of these matches in his *Highways and Byways in East Anglia* (1901). At Burgh, apparently, there was a favourite camping ground for matches between different parishes or hundreds and a nearby area was used for prize-fights with a quick getaway across the river for the fighters should they be disturbed by the police. Three hundred men on each side were said to have taken part in one camping match between Norfolk and Suffolk on Diss Common in the mid-eighteenth century, and Suffolk were declared the winners after fourteen hours of play. Nine men died from this encounter which was called a 'fighting camp', not surprisingly for it was permissible to fell an opponent in any way one cared. A more reasonable game of twelve-a-side was said to be the last played in Norfolk; this was between the representatives of two hundreds in the early nineteenth century. Even so it went on for two hours. Games differed substantially, as far as it is possible to

109

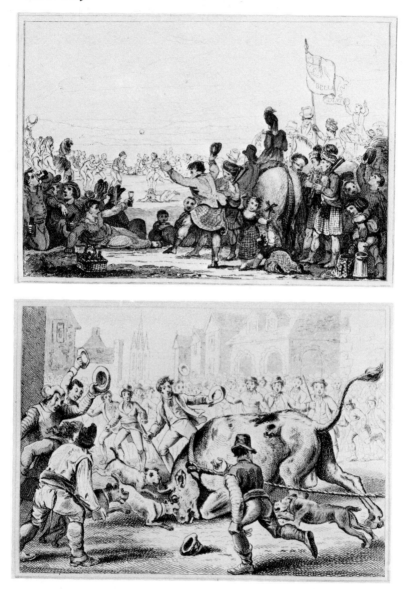

Football w
rough and
uncontrolle
it was enjoy
Scotland as
as England

Bull baiting
bull running
looked forwa
by the bulk o
population. .
towns had a
ring

tell, and in some at least it appeared that the ball was carried and passed from one player to another before being carried between the goal-posts, suggesting that the origins of Rugby football should be sought much further back than is commonly the case.

For the poor these football matches, played all over the country on Shrove Tuesday and on other occasions, replaced the gentlemen's hunting and his 'sprees'. Another rough and tumble, which had an element of danger, was bull-running. In this sport a bull, destined to be slaughtered at the end of the day and its meat distributed to the poor, was allowed to run loose through the streets. Shops and windows were barricaded against damage and side streets were sealed off. The bull was run from one end of the town to another by young men armed with sticks. The fun was in the danger, the general excitement and confusion, with applause for those who showed the greatest daring. Sometimes the bull was baited instead of being run, and permanent bull rings, secured to the ground, could often be found in the centres of towns. The bull, too, was frequently a gift from the town or from a farmer or landlord. By the end of the eighteenth century this sport had declined in favour, not among the poor but among the growing middle class who disliked the savagery and the danger to property. Robert W. Malcolmson, who has shed a great deal of light on eighteenth century play in his book *Popular Recreations in English Society, 1700–1850* (1973), described in detail the battle between the people of Stamford and authority when it was decided to end bull-running in that town. The populace reacted so strongly to the suggestion that they managed to thwart for fifty years the attempts of lords, magistrates, soldiers, constables, and finally the Society for the Prevention of Cruelty to Animals to spoil their sport. * By the end of that time there were few who wished to continue it.

The poor found a champion in William Windham, statesman and MP for Norwich and other places. He was against the attempt to put a stop to bull-baiting and other blood sports enjoyed by the people and he argued, in the House of Commons, that it was strange that persons who had laws to protect their own amusements should want to abolish the sport of the poor on the grounds of cruelty. 'What appearance must we make', he asked, 'if we, who have every source of amusement open to us, and yet follow these cruel sports, become rigid censors of the sports of the poor, and abolish them on account of their cruelty, when they are not more cruel than our own.' Windham, it should be said, on a previous occasion had defended camping because it 'combined all athletic excellencies, a successful combatant requiring to be a good boxer, runner, and wrestler'. The argument over cruel sports and the poor was continued hotly for the first thirty years of the nineteenth century. Gradually it was included in the bigger argument over the *state* of the poor; for consciences were awakening to some realization that the poor in towns were being deprived of almost everything a human being desired while, in the country, they were being left to starve.

---

*The RSPCA was founded in 1824, sixty years before the founding of a society to protect children.

10

☆ *INTERLUDE* ☆

Gaping and marvelling

There was a lot to look and marvel at in the eighteenth century and the Englishman, as always, made indulging his curiosity part of his play, without bothering much to ask himself whether the sight was worth while or the time spent upon it rewarding. For centuries the showman has taken advantage of this weakness by enticing money out of people's pockets in return for creating astonishment and mystery. Thomas Turner wrote: 'In the afternoon my wife walked to Whitesmith, to see a mountybank perform wonders, who has a stage built there, and comes once a week to cuzen a parcel of poor deluded creatures out of their money, by selling his packets, which are to cure people of more distempers than they ever had in their lives . . .' (1760). After the Restoration there were new and more serious marvels turning simple wonder into enchantment through man's scientific magic. The rich and the idle of this time had so much to do in catching up with invention that they could make a brave show of filling in their time. Evelyn and Pepys were a little too early to enjoy half the wonders that the next century was to afford but Evelyn did manage to take a look at Mr Boyle's pneumatic engine performing divers experiments and he greatly admired the ingenuity of Sir Samuel Morland whose inventions—they included pumps, calculating machines and a speaking trumpet—were numerous, varied and practical.

Both diarists loved fireworks, as did everyone else for no event seemed complete without them, or bonfires. Fireworks were already gorgeous with splendid set pieces. Horace Walpole described the fireworks at the peace celebrations in 1749 at Ranelagh, 'which by no means answered the expense', and found them well below his expectations. His comments indicate how sophisticated these displays had become. 'The rockets, and whatever was thrown up into the air, succeeded mighty well; but the wheels, and all that was to compose the principal part, were pitiful and ill-conducted, with no changes of coloured fires and shapes.' Later, Domenico Angelo, a fencing master, was in charge of the fireworks at Ranelagh and was accorded a benefit night on 29 June 1767. He appeared to have deserved it. On a more domestic note Sylas Neville recorded in his diary: 'In the evening fired off some fireworks in the South Garden and some on the pond; serpents ran well upon the ice.'

London was full of curiosities that brightened the daily round when they appeared on show either at the fairs or on some special stand in the streets. Many of these same freaks or acts would be on tour in the summer months and would draw the country folk in the same way. John Evelyn, intellectual though he was, could no more resist the opportunity for viewing the unusual

The wonder of the eighteenth century, the balloon. Everyone, except Horace Walpole, rushed to see one in the sky

A bear and a monkey were still high up in street corner and fair entertainment

than could the barber's wife or the boy returning home from school. A list of things he went out of his way to see included a lion playing with a lamb, a sheep with six legs, a goose with four, a rope-dancer called the Turk, a large whale in the Thames, monkeys and apes at St Margaret's Fair, an Italian woman rope dancer ('all the court went to see her'), the pelicans in St James's Park, a wrestling match for £1000, also in the park, between the western and the northern men in the presence of His Majesty, a gigantic woman (6ft 10in tall), Richardson the famous fire-eater and a fellow who swallowed a knife (in a sheaf of horn) and divers great pebblestones, which rattled one against the other inside him.

Pepys, less unexpectedly, went to see a woman with a beard, in Holborn, and enjoyed it; a tall woman (6ft 5in without shoes—'I measured her') and once on a visit to Bartholomew Fair (he was fond of it) saw 'a poor fellow, whose legs were tied behind his back, dance upon his hands with his arse above his head, and also danced upon his crutches, without any legs upon the ground to help him, which he did with that pain that I was sorry to see it'. He was not convinced, however, that the great baboon from Guiny was a true species. He thought it was a monster 'got of a man and a she-baboon'.

Away in Norfolk Parson Woodforde was also reluctant to miss a good show. He saw a dwarf man, a girl without arms who used her toes as fingers, and a 31-year-old woman who was 33 inches high. One of the most attractive exhibits to him was the learned Pigg, seen at Norwich in 1785. 'After dinner the Captain and myself went and saw the learned Pigg at the *Rampant Horse* in St. Stephens . . . it was wonderful to see the sagacity of the animal. It was a Boar Pigg, very thin, quite black with a Magic Collar on his neck. He would spell any word or number from the letters and figures that were placed before him. Paid for seeing the Pigg 0-1-0.' Woodforde also enjoyed the wonderful feats of horsemanship of Hughes and his children in London, a grand procession at Norwich and the wild beasts of the Tower of London. The Tower of London animals were a regular attraction for Londoners and visitors alike.

The really big wonder of the eighteenth century was the balloon. It was as much a talking point then as space travel has been in the twentieth. Walpole, ready as usual to mock, wrote:

Do not wonder that we do not entirely attend to the things of the earth; fashion has ascended to a higher element. Balloons occupy senators, philosophers, ladies, everybody . . . All this may be very important: to me it looks somewhat foolish. Very early in my life I remember this town at gaze on a man who *flew down* a rope from the top of St Martin's steeple [Violante, an Italian] now, later in my day, people are staring at a voyage to the moon.

He continued in prescient mood:

I hope these new mechanic meteors will prove only playthings for the learned and the idle, and not to be converted into new engines of destruction to the human race, as is so often the case of refinements or discoveries in science. The wicked wit of man always studies to apply the result of talents to enslaving, destroying or cheating his fellow creatures. Could we reach the moon, we should think of reducing it to a province of some European kingdom.

Down at Olney, though much concerned with the celestial, Cowper did not see these evil possibilities. 'My mind', he wrote, 'is frequently getting into these balloons, and is busy in multiplying speculations as airy as the regions through which they pass.' It was the same in Scotland where 'Balloon' Tytler was trying to convert his airy speculations into practical ascents. He drew big crowds and did manage to rise from the ground on an August day in 1784. His success was short lived, as all his successes were.

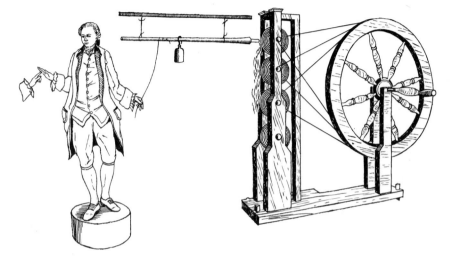

Electricity was a new marvel. Demonstrations of its power and lectures were given at appropriate levels to most walks of society

There was another magic, equally important, not so spectacular but still intriguing. This was electricity, capable of being demonstrated by many delightful experiments in spite of the *Encyclopaedia Britannica* (1st edition, 1768) admitting that it was impossible to define 'because we are entirely ignorant of the nature of the electrical fluid'. Learned men gave lectures with demonstrations to the fashionable at the Royal Society and Herr Katterfelto enthralled the public. According to C. P. Moritz, a German traveller (1782), electricity was the plaything of the English. Certainly remarks like Sylas Neville's, 'He shewed us some Electrical experiments with a new machine and apparatus invented by one Brooke of Norwich' were commonplace. This fascination with electricity calls to mind the evenings spent in the nineteen-twenties listening to the squawks and better sounds coming from home-made wireless sets.

Nor was this all that science made possible for fashionable and other play. There were telescopes and microscopes to look through, and clockwork toys and musical boxes to delight the mind and ear. There was also a new lease of life for puppetry, something which had always been enjoyed but now increased considerably in popularity—even Lady Mary Wortley Montagu enjoyed puppet shows. In the eighteenth century there were both hand and string puppets and plays of all kinds were performed, topical and romantic.

The puppeteers, or motion men, had permanent premises as well as booths at the fairs, and several of them established considerable personal reputations. These men were English but earlier motion men had been Italian, bringing with them the character Punch. However, the now famous Punch and Judy show in more or less its present form dates from 1790.

Other entertainments which made people gather to stand and stare were the infliction of punishments. Very few would be offered the privilege of seeing a man tortured as John Evelyn was in Paris, and such a spectacle was no longer possible in England. Nor were witches executed or put to trial. Nevertheless there were still public hangings, which aroused the same kind of interest as previously and the lesser penalties of sitting in the stocks and being flogged at the cart's tail. When punishment was deserved, as usually it was in the eyes of local communities, the summary justice was applauded and treated as a minor spectacle. No one, not even William Cowper, could see anything inhuman in that. Cowper, in fact, was at his amusing best when describing in a letter the following scene at Olney. A thief had been caught and was to be flogged through the town by the beadle. The beadle had been bribed to treat the thief kindly so the lash of his whip was covered with red ochre to deceive the public into believing that the prisoner was being soundly chastized. When the onlookers discovered the deception they joined the procession, belabouring the beadle who was now compelled to belabour the thief. However, when Parson Woodforde, on another occasion, discovered that a collection was being taken for the hangman, to encourage him to whip soundly an old offender found guilty of stealing potatoes he was disapproving: 'For my part I would not contribute one farthing to it.'

Bartholomew Fair

11

☆ *GENTLEMEN AND PLAYERS* ☆

Into the Victorian Age

'Perplext wi' leisure' the Gentlemen were to remain for forty years yet and some of them for longer. All the same it was already clear that life could never return to the carefree attitudes of the early eighteenth century when other people hardly mattered except as assets to comfort. Nor were country estates and country pleasures, except at certain seasons, the only things on their minds. There were sterner questions of how to make new fortunes from the minerals under the ground or the factories on top of it. Like Sir Leicester Dedlock in *Bleak House*, they remained contemptuous of the industrial revolution but profited by it when or where they could. In more subtle ways other changes were pending. A few gentlemen of unquestionable title—Lord Shaftesbury was the supreme example—interested themselves in the condition of the poor; another group were excited by the possibilities of a more scientific approach to agriculture; but these were still the exceptions, and the belief that the countryside and all things animate and inanimate upon and within it belonged by right to the landed lords and squire was still arrogantly strong. But not quite everywhere: at Wreyland in Devonshire game was preserved by the 1850s but earlier in the century 'game was in abundance' and at times 'all classes of people' were out for a day's sport (Cecil Torr, *Small Talk at Wreyland*).

Often now the big house was closed and the shutters up while the family were abroad or in London for the season, but they were always at home for the shooting, which had a ritual of its own. It had become much easier now to shoot quantities of birds. For one thing the old method of going out with a dog, waiting for him to point, and then shooting the solitary bird had been abandoned in favour of the 'battue', in which the sportsman took up his position and awaited the coming of the birds (and rabbits and hares) flushed from their peacefulness by a line of beaters. As speed was now the essence the gentlemen had loaders who kept them supplied with guns and the fire was more or less continuous. The 'bags' were enormous at many house parties, the hospitality of the host being gauged by the quantity of birds offered to the marksmen. 'Rather stupid,' thought the Reverend B. J. Armstrong, vicar of East Dereham, when he lunched with a party in 1860, 'the conversation all about shooting'.

In theory, after 1831, anyone who could afford to buy a game certificate could shoot game; in practice he had to make himself socially acceptable first, for otherwise he would never be where the game was. Because game was more than ever a social asset, gentlemen spent their money on it, employing gamekeepers to the number required to conserve and preserve,

Cruikshank lists the three Rods and illustrates their activities in inimitable style

supplying the engines of war against vermin in the shape of human and animal-traps, and seeing to it that the rearing of birds for sport was a major part of their occupation to ensure their reputations as sound and good fellows. The gamekeepers were busy. The resentment felt among the poor coincided in many areas with genuine distress. Poachers, therefore, had two incentives, to fill the pot and to outwit the keepers, seen as the enemies of their own people.

As significant as shooting were wagering and gambling on cards and horse racing. No scandal was greater than one aroused by cheating at cards or fixing a race. Both could lead to duels and dishonour. Leaders in this world of fashion, and particularly that of the turf, were two cousins known equally well as sportsmen and politicians. Lord George Bentinck (1802–1848), a son of the fourth Duke of Portland, and Charles Cavendish Fulke Greville (1794–1865), a grandson of a former prime minister, the third Duke of Portland, were social celebrities from choice, flair and birth. Fortunately for posterity Greville kept a diary which, like Trollope's novels, made it plain enough which families ruled and which rules applied to them.

It was hardly possible not to be interested in horse racing if one belonged to these families. Everyone rode and an interest in a stud was an enviable circumstance. Lord George Bentinck was an extreme example of an enthusiast but only because he carried the enthusiasms of his class to greater lengths than others. He owned a string of horses and kept them first at the then famous racing stables at Danebury and later at Goodwood with the Duke of Richmond's trainer. The fifth Duke of Richmond was yet another figure who combined politics with being a peer and a sportsman. No one, however, matched Lord George's ability to be at the heart of rows, scandals and reforms. He it was who invented the horse-box which confounded his opponents when it was first used. Until its invention horses had walked from their stables to the courses, sometimes travelling great distances over many days.

There were other characters. George Osbaldeston (1787–1866), Master of the Quorn and of the Pytchley, was one of them. He fought a duel with Lord

...acing at Epsom. ...he year is 1836 ...nd the sport looks ...tablished and ...ganized

...nything for a ...ager. Squire ...sbaldeston ...acked himself for ...00 guineas to ...de 200 miles in ...nder ten hours. ...e won easily. He ...anged horses ...ery four miles!

Hunting was not so organized as racing, according to the artist Henry Alken, 1813. A huge, competitive field keeping well up with the quarry

George and among his feats was riding 200 miles in 10 hours. That memorable ride—he arranged for a fresh horse every 4 miles—won him a bet of 1000 guineas. He completed the course with 1 hour and 18 minutes to spare. Osbaldeston's knowledge of hounds was said to be unrivalled and he was (*vide* the *Dictionary of National Biography*) 'a great breeder'. His other accomplishments included steeplechasing and playing cricket. He was a justice of the peace, of course.

Another sportsman, Grantley Berkeley (1800–1881), was less aloof. With his brother Moreton he ran the staghounds at Cranford, a village near London, where he was joined for the hunts by a miscellaneous crew far removed in social status from the members of other hunts in the shires. The stags were as urbanized as their pursuers. When hard pressed they took to hiding in barns in preference to making for the open country. Farmers greatly objected to Grantley Berkeley's hunt, sought compensation for damage done and finally drove its master to Oakley in Bedfordshire and the foxhounds there. But not for long; he was soon quarrelling again, challenging one of the Whitbreads, a distinguished Bedfordshire family, to a duel in the process.

There were also the hunting parsons. They were to be found everywhere, although not all parsons hunted. One of the more famous was the Reverend 'Jack' Russell of the west country. (The Bishops of Exeter had a particularly difficult time with their sporting clerics.) Much beloved as a parish priest, with a faithful and admiring following, Russell hunted as often as possible and too frequently for his pocket. He was credited with having spent £50,000 of his wife's money on the sport, although it was probably a gift to him as she hunted almost as often as he did. The hunting parsons were no enigmas.

Often the younger offspring of the great houses, they had been brought up to hunt, shoot and fish like the eldest brothers. So long as the fathers were alive there were no financial difficulties: they were bought commissions in the army or livings in the church, with the object of continuing gentlemen's lives for as long as possible. When the fathers died most of the money went with the estates to the eldest sons who, by this time usually had sons of their own. It was accepted bad luck that deprived many parsons of the way of life to which they had been brought up.

A footnote to the love of hunting at this time is that it gave the fox a better chance. Before the Reverend 'Jack' had established his pack by convincing Devon farmers and villagers that the way to deal with foxes was to leave them to the hunt, a more ruthless method of execution had been adopted. This was to trace the fox to its earth; then the church bells were rung and as many men as wished gathered with their weapons. First they dug the fox out, then they slaughtered it as vermin.

Meanwhile the ladies, especially those in towns, were busy developing the more gracious play of social life and spending almost as much money on it as their husbands did on sport. Their play was to surpass, or equal if surpassing was impossible, the balls and parties of those they considered to be their rivals. They were following the tradition set by the ladies of Almack's who in the early years of the century managed the balls at those assembly rooms and ensured that no one below the proper station obtained a card of admission. Soon every stratum of society had its balls and dinner parties and the formality of these evening events was pronounced. Many books were published on etiquette to help the aspiring and the nervous, particularly those whose families were new to the importance of the niceties of dress, deportment and general behaviour on special occasions. By 1860 *Enquire Within Upon Everything* had reached its 14th edition, and sold 146,000

A quadrille danced at the famous Almack's with Lady Worcester having her hand kissed but not by Lord Worcester who is on the left

copies. It was filled with information and advice on just those points that could ruin pleasure on social occasions, from how to prevent the smoking of a lamp to running a ball and comporting oneself well at it. It was a best seller in suburbia, for every effort was made there to reach the standards of the most famous hostesses. Some of the advice on balls was as follows. An invitation to a ball should be given *at least* a week beforehand. Appear in full dress. Always wear gloves. Do not wear rings on the outside of your gloves. Distribute your attentions as much as possible. Be cordial when serving refreshments but not importunate. In leaving a large party it is unnecessary to bid farewell, and improper to do so before the guests. A Paris card of invitation to an evening party usually implies that you are invited for the season. In balls and large parties there should be a table for cards, and two packs of cards placed upon each table. Chess and all unsociable games should be avoided. Stakes agreed to at parties should be very trifling, so as not to create excitement or discussion. If you have a hobby, keep it to yourself.

In spite of the balls, the receptions, the dinner parties, the theatre-going, the concerts and the music of Johann Strauss, the sense of fun and relaxation was more and more missing from society the longer the reign of Queen Victoria went on. The American Minister in London put it down to the importance of social position. Everything that could be afforded must be utilized to maintain status, he said. Probably he was only half right in this all-American opinion of English life, but the seriousness of life at court was also having its effect. It was summed up by the Prince Consort when discussing the education of the Prince of Wales: its aim was to make the Prince as different as possible from his great uncles. Naughtiness, if any, was to be covered up.

That Victorian seriousness and sense of importance was mirrored in the Great Exhibition of 1851 and in the new attitudes towards education. The reformed public schools were the work of Dr Thomas Arnold. He saw them in much the same terms as the Schools' Inquiry Commission of 1868, places for the sons of well-to-do parents or sons of well-educated parents of confined means. These were the natural leaders of society and needed to be educated to take their place. Dr Arnold was not the only headmaster of his generation to bring schools out of their disrepute and make them into a welcomed influence for good throughout the country; but he was unquestionably the greatest. He went to Rugby School as headmaster in 1828. He knew what his task was: to change a brutal and brutalizing establishment—no worse, of course, and perhaps better than other schools of similar status—into a place of scholarship and Christian behaviour. He so succeeded that before long his boys were not only remarked upon at their universities for their almost unrivalled sense of responsibility but his younger masters who became headmasters were equally successful elsewhere.

Because games played a big part in the training of boys at public boarding schools in later years, it was often assumed that Arnold was a keen believer in the value of sport as a moulder of character. This was not the case. Arnold was fond of games and exercise but they played no part in his theories of education, although it was only natural that at Rugby they became better controlled during his headmastership. Later headmasters did see their value, particularly for boarding schools with many daytime hours to fill. Arnold, in fact, went to Rugby five years after William Webb Ellis 'with a fine disregard for the rules of football as played in his time first took the ball in his arms and ran with it'. This was in 1823, and the words are from the plaque put up many years after the event, but what Ellis did sounds not unlike the camping game in East Anglia which he may have heard of or even seen. How the game was played at Rugby in Arnold's time is splendidly described in *Tom Brown's Schooldays*, the author, Thomas Hughes, having been at the school from 1834 to 1842.

Rugby football. There are now limits to the field of play and rules as Tom Brown's friend explains

The first match Tom saw was between school-house and the rest of the school: fifty or sixty in one team and an unpredictable number on the other. The bounds were set by the gravel walk on the one side and the line of elms on the other. When the ball crossed the bounds it was said to be 'in touch'. When a player put the ball down behind the line (if not prevented by a crowd of smaller boys posted there to prevent him) he earned the right for his side to have a 'try' at goal. From touch, as today, there was a line-out. 'Ain't there just fine scrummages then!', scrummages being a toiling mass of bodies and legs. Although the players were unaware of it they were establishing, as they toiled, the right of gentlemen to take part in physical contact games; very soon now boys would continue to play football games after leaving school and college. Their homes were not necessarily in the country; many were sons of merchants and industrialists. Field sports were unknown to many and the next step in order to continue playing football was to teach others, not in their class, to play. One other point of interest in Tom's first sight of Rugby football was that the match was for the 'best of three goals: whichever side kicks two goals wins'. This was a continuation of eighteenth-century practice when before the start of a match the terms had to be decided on and the stakes laid. *

When he arrived, Tom saw in the study of his new friend, East, a cricket bat, a fishing rod and irons for climbing trees. There were also pin-ups of dogs' heads, 'Grimaldi winning the Aylesbury steeple-chase, Amy Robsart, the reigning Waverley beauty, and Tom Crib [the boxer] in a posture of defence'.† Outside in the school grounds Tom mentioned the fives courts, already the scene of arranged fights. Nevertheless there was still much free time, always a source of trouble, and boys roamed the countryside, bird-nesting and poaching. And still nothing was more important, annually, than the Derby lottery, excused with the remark that what else could one expect when adults were similarly engaged.

The growth of the middle classes meant a big increase in the demand for public school education. New schools were founded and old ones enlarged. Urbanization also led to a greater interest in organized sport. By the middle of the century the sports and recreations of older boys and girls, often illustrated with pictures of young men and women, were well described in a number of attractive books especially produced for them. Three of these were *Every Boy's Book* (first published 1856; in 1876 its 12th edition had 800 pages), *Every Girl's Book* (first published 1860) and *The Boy's Prize Book of Sports, Games, Exercises and Pursuits* (published first in 1866 and compiled by writers of the *Boy's Own Magazine*). Some of the pastimes described were children's games but the sports which were to be continued into manhood got full treatment. The boys undoubtedly had the best of it; girls still had to wait some years for permission to exert themselves and for the costumes to enable them to do so. Rules for games had not yet been codified so authors aired their prejudices. The author of the entry on football in *The Boy's Prize Book* favoured 'the old leather ball dilated with a good ox-bladder' because the 'newly invented vulcanized India-rubber balls' were liable to cause trouble, an accidental prick or cut rendering them quite useless. He was also against 'mauling', 'hacking', and 'tripping'. For this reason he advised against the Rugby game, 'frequently a barbarous pastime', dismissed the Eton game and favoured Harrow.

Both boys' books included articles on angling, archery, cricket, croquet, football, gymnastics (in favour now for several decades), hockey, riding, rowing, skating and swimming. Croquet was important because it gave a rare opportunity for young men and women to play together; it was played in the 1860s through hoops of wire much closer to the ground than they were later on. Hockey was still primitive. It was described in *The Boy's Prize Book* as suitable for 'a bitter cold day' and was more like a field game of ice-hockey,

---

*School-house boys wore white trousers in this match and the author commented (writing in 1857) that there was none of the colour and tastiness of get-up . . . which lends such life to the present game at Rugby, making the dullest and worst-fought match a pretty sight. By then each house had its own uniform of plush cap and jersey, of some lively colour.

†Pin-ups had been favoured for a number of years. The girls were aristocratic beauties, fully clothed. In London, and probably elsewhere, they adorned the rooms of young men of all classes.

played with a bung for a ball on hard flat ground. Any number could play, providing there was an equal number on each side and the field was large enough.

The *Prize Book* also confirmed in innocent social commentary that cricket was not a prerogative of either 'gentlemen' or 'players'. It was truly 'national'. 'Kings and little princes play at it; paupers and ragged-school boys, out on their annual holidays, play at it. Under the reformed system, the hair-brained inhabitants of Colney Hatch and Hanwell play cricket.'

Swimming was also regarded as very important. Several pages were devoted to it and many drawings of naked boys illustrated the strokes and leg movements, as they did, but not as attractively, in the Reverend J. G. Wood's *Athletic Sports and Recreations for Boys* (1861). The willingness to illustrate swimming with lively pictures of naked boys slightly surprises when it is remembered what an ordeal it was for the ladies of Cambridge, twenty years later, to row through the 'dangerous straits' of the bathing sheds.* But not every bit of the anatomy was shown.

All the books gave space to gymnastics. In one it was called the education of the muscles; in another, the means of making men bright, and vigorous, and ruddy. Dumb-bells and clubs were recommended. There were pictures of the pole vault. Two of the books included driving among the necessary accomplishments of young gentlemen. Skating was 'a recompense for our inability to fly'. Fencing was a required art. *Every Boy's Book* introduced the subject with quotations from the opinions of no fewer than four eminent physicians.

By the 1860s it had been established beyond doubt that athletic exercise in its many forms was to be included among the proper accomplishments of urban gentlemen, which word now embraced all those whose parents had been able to pay for their extended education; in other words, it was at last possible, just, to be a gentleman without owning land. In consequence the great games-playing era was about to begin and to spread to all classes before a decline set in one hundred years later. Meanwhile the ladies were about to make a start.

It was not much of a start. The illustrations in *Every Boy's Book*, apart from the early chapters on playground and indoor games, showed young men and women and not boys and girls. Women were seen in the illustrations accompanying the articles on archery, croquet and riding in an active role; and a passive one in driving. *Every Girl's Book* ignored outside games and concentrated on dozens of petty games invented to kill time. That was Part I. Part II was entitled 'Ladies' Work'. It was a short part indicating clearly what the ladies were supposed to be doing while the men were out enjoying themselves. There was embroidery in chenille, flowers in chenille, embroidery in feathers, embroidery in coloured silks, in gold, raised embroidery, embroidery in narrow ribbons, flowers from Berlin wool, knitted moss for mats, flowers from goose-feathers, Madeira feather-flowers, artificial flowers, wax flowers, wax fruit, ornamental leather work,

---

*Information from that lovely book of memories and drawings, *Period Piece* by Gwen Raverat.

potichomanie, * diaphanie or stained glass, painting upon glass, imitation ground glass, oriental tinting, painting on silk or velvet, blinds or transparencies in oriental tinting, Chinese lacquer-work, French lacquer-work, coral baskets and firepapers. Stove-aprons were made as follows:

> ... cut out the various leaves and flowers with a sharp pair of scissors, and arrange them in such a wreath or group as suits your fancy on your square of black net, gumming them firmly to it. Stretch your net over a light wooden framework, or, prettier still, fasten it into a square frame of plain gold beading, fix it into your fireplace, and you have, at the most trifling cost of trouble and expense, a really elegant and useful article of furniture. †

This genteel living for ladies of the middle classes, resident mainly in the towns and suburbia, descended on them about the time of the wedding of Queen Victoria to her cousin Albert (1840). It was a large albatross about their necks. Games did at least help to get rid of it, and at the same time enabled young ladies to rediscover their legs.

Meantime in the drawing rooms, when 'work' was done, there was much playing of parlour games, of making music, of reciting, of reading aloud, an accomplishment of equal importance to performing competently on the pianoforte. One primer, *The Modern Reader and Speaker: a selection of Poetry and Prose from the writing of eminent authors with copious extracts for Recitation; preceded by the Principles of Elocution comprising a Variety of Exercises, from the simplest articulation to the Utmost extent of vocal expression: with a system of Gesture, illustrated by diagrams and a plan of Notation* was published before 1850 and in its 23rd edition by 1866. That edition had 448 pages. Twentieth-century woman would get most amusement from the first twenty pages of the second part entitled *Expressive Management of the Body*; 'Principles of Gesture' began with the feet and lower limbs (no legs in this book) and ended with the head and countenance.

Boys and young men contributed to drawing-room entertainment by singing with the girls and showing them conjuring tricks and simple scientific experiments, the girls responding with wonder and delight. This kind of evening entertainment lasted until the outbreak of World War I.

In the country, and in the fields surrounding the towns, there was a new interest in natural history collections, stuffed birds, birds' eggs, butterflies and flowers. The girls collected the flowers and pressed them, or made paintings of them in their albums. The boys collected the eggs and anything that required killing. There was a race of men, mostly country vicars, who, under the influence of Gilbert White and Bewick, took delight in observing nature, but mostly men were still concerned to kill. David J. Armitage in a pamphlet *Birds and Man* (1972) collected some depressing facts about the disappearance of breeding species from Britain during the 1880s. Part of the disappearance was attributable to new farming methods but most was the

---

*According to the Shorter OED *potichomania*, 1855, was the craze for imitating Japanese or other porcelain by covering the inner surface of glass vessels etc, with designs on paper or sheet gelatine.

†It may have no significance but the author's copy of *Every Boy's Book* barely hangs together, whereas the *Girl's* is as bright and as good as new.

48. Continuative Motions.

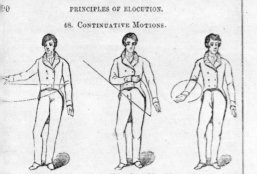

(Motion 10.)—*Diag.* 21.   (Motion 11.)—*Diag.* 22.   (Motion 12.)—*Diag.* 23.

Motion 10. A horizontal movement. (Diagram 21.)

Motion 11. Commences at *elevated extended*, marks its accent on *downwards across*, rebounds to *horizontal across*. (Diagram 22.)

Motion 12. A circular movement, the hand supine—generally performed by a motion of the wrist. (Diagram 23.)

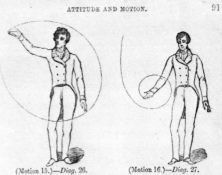

(Motion 15.)—*Diag.* 26.   (Motion 16.)—*Diag.* 27.

Motion 15. A circular movement commencing at *horizontal oblique*, sweeping downwards, inwards, outwards, and upwards, ending in *elevated oblique*. (Diagram 26.)

Motion 16. Returns the hand from *elevated oblique*, by a circular movement, and ends in *downwards oblique*. By this, the hand is generally returned from every *elevated* point on the right side. (Diagram 27.)

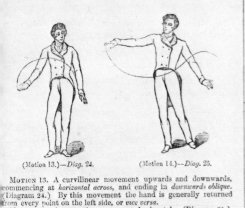

(Motion 13.)—*Diag.* 24.   (Motion 14.)—*Diag.* 25.

Motion 13. A curvilinear movement upwards and downwards, commencing at *horizontal across*, and ending in *downwards oblique*. (Diagram 24.) By this movement the hand is generally returned from every point on the left side, or *vice versa*.

Motion 14. A serpentine movement, horizontal. (Diagram 25.)

(Motion 17.)—*Diag.* 28.   (Motion 18.)—*Diag.* 29.

Motion 17. A curvilinear movement, commencing at *downwards across*, sweeping downwards, outwards, and upwards, ending in *elevated oblique*. (Diagram 28.)

Motion 18. A circular movement, commencing at *elevated oblique*, sweeping upwards, inwards, downwards, and outwards, ending in *elevated extended*. (Diagram 29.)

How to make your recital or speech interesting: the principles of elocution

---

work of gamekeepers, of casual sportsmen with their guns, and of the egg collector. The Great Bustard in its final retreat in East Anglia was hunted by hounds. Keepers on an estate in the Scottish Highlands added up their total three-year bag from Whit Sunday 1837 to Whit Sunday 1840 and found it to be: 27 white tailed sea eagles, 15 golden eagles, 18 ospreys, 98 blue hawks (peregrine falcons), 275 kites (salmon tailed gleads), 5 march harriers, 63 goshawks, 7 orange-legged falcons, 11 hobby hawks, 285 common buzzards. 3 honey buzzards, 462 kestrels or red hawks, 78 merlin hawks, 9 ash-coloured hawks, 83 hen harriers, 6 jer falcons, 1341 carrion hooded crows, 475 ravens, 35 horned owls, 71 common fern owls (nightjars?), 3 golden owls and 8 magpies. Tom Brown, it will be recalled, added his bit by climbing the tree to reach the kestrel's nest and obtaining all but one of the eggs—considered a smart piece of work because the climb was difficult and the eggs rare. Later on in the century man discovered Africa and began his years of extermination there.

The theatre suffered badly in this period and was hardly considered by suburbia as a proper place to be seen. On the other hand the Reverend B. J. Armstrong, up from East Dereham, took his children to the Marionette Theatre in London in 1852 ('the deception was really admirable'), saw Kean 'and wife' in *The Winter's Tale* in 1856, and delighted in the pantomime at Drury Lane with its cascade of real water. Kean, Henry Irving and Ellen Terry were all acting but the last two reserved their greatest triumphs for later decades. For the time being, the climate of opinion was against them. Melodramatic plays were generally poor, while the realism that was sweeping Europe hardly found a British playwright capable of handling it, with the exception of T. W. Robertson who wrote several good plays of the kind in the sixties, helped, as were so many others in the theatrical profession, by Sir Squire and Lady Bancroft.

In the big houses it was a rather different story. Amateur dramatics were very much the thing and those with a real or supposed gift for acting almost specialized in the kind of house party that included dramatics. 'Do you know Mary Boyle—daughter of the old Admiral?' Dickens enquired of Sir Edward Bulwer Lytton in 1850, 'because she is the very best actress I ever saw off the stage, and immeasurably better than a great many I have seen on it. I have acted with her in a country house in Northamptonshire, and am going to do so again next November. If you know her, I think she would be more than pleased to play . . .'

This period, from the great Reform Bill to 1870, was quite remarkable for its discovery of the poor and the realization that something had got to be done about their leisure, particularly in towns. The leisure they had was little enough but, when it came, almost the only pleasure open to them in the 1830s was to drink; by 1870, although drinking was still a major occupation, other forms of amusement were available. Many famous names spring to mind among the reformers who contributed during this time to the betterment of the state of the poor. Those finding it easiest to win a hearing were men and women who insisted that without education the poor would be left in a state of brutality. Others approached the problem from the point of view of health. Among these was a little known Scottish doctor, John Hogg, who came to London in the twenties to take up a hospital appointment and felt moved to write a book, *London as it is; being a series of observations on the Health, Habits, and Amusements of the People* (1837). It was a splendidly detailed analysis and in conclusion offered suggestions for leading the people away from intoxication to temperance by offering them other things to do. It found the kernel of the problem 'in the distance maintained by the upper classes between themselves and those beneath them'. The poor were even excluded 'from exhibitions and scenes calculated to elevate and improve the mind' because these were always shut when they were at liberty to go or because payment had to be made. At Westminster Abbey, for example, there was a payment to go in and further payments to enter different portions of the building. Worse still, if one entered the building free during service time in the nave it was necessary to leave after the service or pay to remain. Dr Hogg quoted some stanzas from *Frazer's Magazine* (1831) of which the concluding one was:

I thought of Blenheim—when at once upon my startl'd ear
There came a sound—it chill'd my veins, it froze my heart with fear
As from a wild unearthly voice I heard those accents drop—
'Sarvice is done—'tis tuppence now for them as vants to stop.'

He remarked also on the hours of opening at the British Museum 'from which it would appear that the doors were purposely closed against the lower classes'.

He wrote next of the shortage of greens for cricket or football play and argued against those who wanted Sunday to be a 'day of humiliation rather than rejoicing'. The upper classes seemed to think that it was all right for them to listen to a military band on Sunday afternoons or to visit the animals in the Zoological Gardens 'and no one challenges the propriety of *their* conduct'. Happily, and almost before the ink was dry on his quill, improvements had begun to take place and the great movement for the enlightenment, if not for the amusement of the poor, had begun. In fact the Municipal Reform Act of 1835, which established local councils elected by ratepayers, gave these local authorities powers to raise money to provide the means for improving the moral, mental and physical state of the masses. Nothing much happened until 1850 as far as recreational facilities were concerned, but in that year The Public Libraries and Museums Act was passed and before 1870 some authorities had taken advantage of it and of the Recreation Grounds Act of 1859. It was a revolution, though the fruits of it were not clearly visible in most places until later in the century.

It was the public lecture that attracted many societies as a means of instructing and humanizing the masses. Fortunately they were not all dull. The Reverend B. J. Armstrong mentioned one he went to in London given by Albert Smith on the Ascent of Mont Blanc (1853). It was a humorous lecture with a real St Bernard dog 'and a panorama very prettily painted'. Also in London (1857) he heard Gordon Cumming the lion hunter, half of whose exploits he clearly did not believe. Back at East Dereham a lecture in the Assembly Rooms on The Dark Side of London (1859) attracted a large crowd of working classes and later in the same year there was a conversazione in the town hall, 'the object being to show goodwill to the lower classes by mingling with them'. But if Armstrong accepted 'station in life' as the natural order he was sympathetic towards the poor and critical of his equals. He disliked the gentry's 'idling of time'. 'People have no right to twaddle a precious morning away at bagatelle or in insipid and profitless conversation.' He himself went annually on choir outings, usually to Norwich; he reported that a farmer, Mr Overman, took forty of his men to Lowestoft for an outing; and he rejoiced that the wonderful art of photography had made it possible for cottagers to have sixpenny likenesses of their sons in the army or their daughters in service. He, himself, enjoyed simple amusements: he thought the Crystal Palace a fairyland; he described street amusements in London including canaries dancing on a rope; he watched skaters on the Serpentine—thousands of them, with here and there a woman—and at Berkhamsted, where his in-laws lived, he went to the Oddfellows Grand Annual Fête (1860) and saw with amusement how the girls chose the Rifle Volunteers in a gigantic kiss-in-the-ring. Most people, he said, behaved

(above) Before they were allowed to rediscover their legs the ladies loved archery. It brought them the company of men and many were good at it

(below) Skating mid century in Hyde Park. Gentlemen sat down to have their skates fitted

much better than would have been possible a few years back.

More important, perhaps, football was at last being organized. Of the clubs now playing in the English Football League Notts County was founded in 1862 and the Football Association itself in 1863. At that date not much more had been established than that a football team was, when conveniently possible, composed of eleven players. Even the size of the ball was a matter of controversy and the rules governing play were almost as various as the number of clubs playing. One peculiar difficulty was that the game in the south was largely a gentleman's game of Old Boys' Clubs connected with well-known public schools, whereas in the north it was a players' game, sometimes organized with the help of gentlemen connected with Sunday schools and boys' clubs, and sometimes growing out of factory life. Play was savage. Until the new ideals of the public schools took over, it was supposed to be savage, an opportunity for the young, to use a new industrial metaphor, to let off steam. At this time, it was said, matches would sometimes continue although the ball had been lost. All the early pictures show matches being played without idea of positioning. Like little boys today the players charged after the ball in a pack getting their enjoyment from the maul or the chase.

That kind of behaviour was useless for competitive play and it was competition that the Football Association wished to promote. So the long battle began over agreeing on rules and making the game more orderly. It was not easy for, in the first place, not everyone was ready to accept the authority of a central body and, in the second, the game was not yet dissociated entirely from the Rugby game. Yorkshire meanwhile formed an Association of its own and drafted rules. Fortunately it was not the only strong area outside London. Birmingham was important and, in Scotland, Glasgow.

Two other competitive sports, cricket and rowing, were more advanced in organization and public favour. There was cricket everywhere, in villages, in towns, in counties. All the present first class counties had an organization before 1870, although several only managed it after 1860. Yorkshire was one of the late ones although there had been cricket in plenty in the county for decades. The present minor counties were also well organized at an early date but the names of the strongest counties at the end of the sixties had a familiar

ord's Cricket
round and
entlemen v
layers. Scorers
w have a high
dder and a score
oard

The Oxford boat race crew in training, 1881. The gentleman on the horse is the coach. He would ride a bicycle today

ring. They were Surrey, Nottinghamshire, Middlesex and Yorkshire. The gentlemen dominated the game and had made the rules, but everyone played.

Interest in rowing had begun with the annual race for Thames watermen, Doggett's Coat and Badge, instituted in 1716 in honour of the accession of George I by Thomas Doggett, an actor famous for his interpretation of comic parts. But the livery was awarded not so much to encourage rowing as to encourage the watermen whose services were vital to London's communications. Another hundred years had to pass before the next important event, which was Oxford's defeat of Cambridge at Henley in 1829. Cambridge had started their own head of the river races (the Mays) in 1827 and earlier still, in 1817, the Leander Club had been formed. The Wingfield Sculls started on the Thames in 1830, Henley Royal Regatta began with a Grand Challenge Cup for eights in 1839, and most of the other familiar Henley races were started in the forties. Regattas were common at seaside resorts, as they were in the United States, and in England the King's Cup for yacht racing was established in 1827, to become the Queen's Cup in 1838. Many new rowing and yachting clubs were active after 1850. It was all rather snobbish but at least it was a spectator sport which poorer people could and did enjoy.

Coursing was another activity to leap ahead in public appreciation in the 1830s when the Waterloo Cup was established. It had been popular for centuries, the first known rules (the laws of the leash) being compiled in Queen Elizabeth I's reign. The National Coursing Club was founded in 1858. Coursing was fine for gambling, as was steeplechasing, the Grand National

Steeplechase being run for the first time in 1837 and transferred to Aintree in 1839. The early days of steeplechasing, actually so called because in early matches a steeple would often be the mark for the line, were full of exciting incident and famous names of horses and men. The sport began in the eighteenth century in Ireland, when a man would lead over the countryside for a wager, continuing until his horse fell or his opponent was unable to follow. In England the first course of manufactured fences was at Bedford in 1810 but it was not until after 1830 that numbers of meetings were held, usually in March and April. The popularity of steeplechasing continued to grow, then declined, but was fully restored to favour in 1870.

By that year also all sport was prospering and nearly every game was being organized for match play. Croquet had long been popular on vicarage and country-house lawns. It continued to be so but in 1867 a men's championship was started, to be followed only two years later by a championship for women. Other championships were for golf (not ladies'), played at Prestwick during the sixties, and the Queen's Prize for target-shooting with the service rifle, which was won initially in 1860 by Private Ross. A new sport as far as records were concerned was mountaineering. Peaks had been scaled at much earlier dates but the 1860s produced an avalanche of firsts. Tennis (not lawn) had had champions for many years but even that ancient game started in 1867 a new competition for the gold and silver rackets.

Something to do and something to watch. Even the smallest towns now looked forward to travelling menageries and theatre companies at regular intervals, as well as their usual fairs. The Ethopian singers went twice to Southwold and gave two performances on one day there at the height of their popularity as singers of American slave songs (1847). There were many concerts and brassband performances. Some people managed to see the wondrous Lestard on his flying trapeze. Everyone was always looking forward to the next event. It was the railway age and one really had to live in remote parts not to benefit.

Croquet on the lawn for a family party, 1865. Note the small hoops

12

☆ *TOWN PLAYERS 1870–1914* ☆

By 1870 industry had appreciated that supplying games players with their implements of enjoyment was likely to be big business and firms had been founded to manufacture equipment. Because of the size of the growing market, research became profitable and from then on bats, rackets, sticks and clubs began to have a modern look. Billiards, for example, had been a fashionable pastime for several centuries but the table had had imperfections. John Thurston's firm, founded in 1799, introduced in the next half-century first rubber, then vulcanized rubber, cushions to improve play. But the table itself, of marble and wood, was seldom really true and it was with some pride that in *The Art Journal Illustrated Catalogue of the Great Exhibition, 1851,* Thurston was able to announce the substitution of slate tops for wood. Already public billiard rooms were in existence and as the years went by they increased by hundreds. Naturally enough *The Art Journal Catalogue* had few items of sporting equipment in its pages but it is noticeable that the rivalry between manufacturers of phaetons was intense and fully equalled the competition between manufacturers of motor cars today; moreover, styling was, if anything, even more important.

New materials also affected the popularity of a game. Golf was a good example of this. Its long history, in Scotland particularly, and its most famous clubs the Royal and Ancient and the Royal Blackheath, both founded in the eighteenth century, confirmed that it was a good game; nevertheless it had a limitation placed upon its popularity by the unsatisfactory nature of the ball. Like those used for some other games it was made of leather stuffed with feathers and sewn. Hitting a ball of this kind, without the advantage of a wall to play against or an opponent to hit it back, lacked excitement; in addition it had to be kept dry for it disintegrated in the wet and in Scotland and England it was often wet, then as now. Nevertheless the game attracted some fine club-makers at the beginning of the nineteenth century and there were already drivers, spoons, irons and putters when the first gutta-percha ball was tried (1845). 'Paterson's Patent' it was, the Reverend Paterson in fact, and the game was revolutionized after makers had discovered that indentations were needed to improve the flight. The ball forced another change. Previous to its invention courses had settled down, after various numbers had been tried, to nine holes. But eighteen were played by the simple expedient of playing an outward nine and an inward nine, keeping as far as possible on one side of the course. Greens were shared, the 'out' players having precedence, if need be. Now courses had to be eighteen holes because of the length of the drive, and with the arrival of the rubber ball in the new

Golf, the ball teed on sand, as it was until much later. The caddies have no bags to hold the clubs

century another 25 yards was not too much to expect.

Rubber played a big part in the development of many games. It was used, for example, in the football bladder, the cricket handle, and the baseball ball which, unlike balls for rackets and fives, had its cork centre cushioned with rubber before being wound with yarn. Rubber also gave, in the nineteenth century, the opportunity to invent one of the twentieth century's most attractive indoor games, squash rackets. As soft ball was to baseball so squash was to rackets. Both gave opportunity to play a good game at less cost in a smaller area. But the biggest boon of all from rubber was its use for the lawn tennis ball. Without it Major Wingfield's game could not have been popularized and could not have developed into the first really important social ball game.

So with better balls, better rackets, better clubs, better rods with reels, and even a canvas bag to carry golf clubs in instead of tucking them under the arm, men and women made peace with urban living as soon as public courts and grounds were put at their disposal. Moreover they countered the grime of cities by copying the schools in the use of sporting colours. This was the great period for the coloured shirt, the multicoloured scarf, cap and blazer and, in summer, the coloured band to put around a straw boater.* It was not quite the time for more functional clothing. Ladies still played their games, or most of them—not hockey—with absent legs, men wore their shorts long and long white trousers for boating and lawn tennis. This mode of

---

*Until recently, if not still, white-haired gentlemen appeared on the towing path at Henley—some even at Waterloo station—wearing their rowing caps of forty or fifty years ago. An enchanting sight, nearly as good as the Changing of the Guard for the tourist.

dress had its compensations for it was possible to be, or at least to feel, elegant. It was also the era of hero worship: postcards of actors and actresses were in great demand; W. G. Grace was a public figure; and hundreds of young men who got their 'blue', particularly for rowing, could expect adulation at any party.

To make the most of all this euphoria more clubs and associations had to be formed, football and cricket leagues established to promote healthy competition, stadiums built to house masses of enthusiastic supporters, courts and pitches supplied to enable thousands to play, professionalism encouraged to improve standards by coaching and example, and newspaper reporting and specialist magazines developed to feed the minds and reduce the tedium of the long working week before Saturday came again. It was a revolution, accomplished in the main in less than fifty years, but it could not have come about so quickly had not a parallel revolution in public transport taken place. The real motor car age had not begun for the general public, but trains ran everywhere, and even journeys abroad were not considered impossible.

Club teams were of every kind; town clubs, village clubs, works' clubs, Old Boys' clubs, Bank clubs, and wandering clubs with no grounds of their own. For the whole of this period there was still amusement centred in the home, particularly in the winter, but no one now thought of confining their enjoyments to a small circle of friends. Rather they had the best of both worlds, and particularly the less well off who maintained a strong family life and at the same time joined WEA classes and church groups to increase their interests and their circle of friends. Often they joined together to form a rambling club, a cycling club, a literary society, a musical society, or for sport. Sometimes they combined these activities. *

Play also played a big part in women's emancipation. By Edwardian times they were to be seen on the river in boats, often rowing as well as looking decorative, playing tennis on public as well as private courts, and going for bicycle rides and picnics with other girls and men. It was possible at last, at least among the lower and middle parts of the middle classes, to act naturally and to have a jolly time. Judging by her diary of 'doings', the author's mother was certainly successful. Finding herself as a young mother and wife in the freer atmosphere of a London suburb after an upbringing in Lincolnshire, she made the most of it. In the four or five years preceding World War I she had one part-time mother's help whose appearance often heralded the immediate disappearance of herself up to town. Theatre matinées, tea at the Popular, bus rides, tennis on the common or walking with her husband in Richmond Park or on Wimbledon Common were her ideas of play apart from music at home. She tried not to miss anything and waited a long time at Ranelagh to see Kaiser Wilhelm in London for the funeral of King Edward. When the Lyric Theatre, Hammersmith, was

---

*The author's friend W. Garrard (b.1885) joined a London suburban church and with other members formed The Moochers, a literary rambling club. It was led by Will Kent, well known later as an historian of London. Each member had a name according to his talent and Garrard's was Orpheus. Subsequently he won an evening music scholarship and sang at fashionable soirées and in many church choirs.

At the end of the Victorian Age these ladies are still in long skirts, but at least they are outside and playing with skill and vigour

Ping-pong with a long handled bat and spectators all around. It is a long way yet to table tennis

Battledore and shuttlecock, a suitable activity for young ladies. Some felt it had limitations

re-opened after the war by Nigel Playfair the children began their years of sitting on stools for the pit. She believed wholeheartedly that it was better to go to the theatre twenty times a year in the pit than five times in the stalls. She also had to make provision for Sunday concerts at the Albert Hall, very high up.

It was still the age of the amateur: the great age. The professional had his place, provided he came out of another gate from the pavilion at Lord's and was a good fellow. This was particularly the case at cricket which, at the top, had now become so much a gentleman's game that the professional was bound to conform. That the captain of a county team should be an amateur was not even discussed and it caused no embarrassment for there were always many good amateurs ready to play and rich enough to make it easy for them to do so. At football it was not the same story. On the whole amateurs played in one team and the professionals in another. For some time there was little to choose between them except that the number of good professional teams greatly exceeded the good amateur ones. Arsenal, formed in 1886, turned professional in 1891; Aston Villa, formed in 1874, turned professional in 1885; Sheffield Wednesday, formed in 1867, turned professional in 1887; Tottenham Hotspur, formed in 1882, turned professional in 1895. Eventually only the Corinthians among the amateur clubs attempted to remain in the same footballing class as the top professionals. Amateurs, of course, continued to play in the professional teams but the number who were so inclined, or good enough, became fewer and fewer and when training in the best teams became of great importance they dropped out altogether. Grounds were the difficulty. Practically all the famous clubs of today had other grounds before they reached their present homes. Everton (formed 1878) were first at Stanley Park, then at Priory Road, then at Anfield Road, and finally, 1892, at Goodison Park; Leicester City (formed 1884) were at Victoria Park, then at Belgrave Road, then at Victoria Park, and finally, 1891, at Filbert Street. Football, naturally enough since it had been for centuries a poor man's game, was never deeply imbued with the public school spirit. As early as the 1880s football players were going north to Scotland to obtain payment for their skill. In 1885 the professionals' position in England was regularized and, very shortly afterwards, most of the big clubs turned professional.

The Football Association Cup antedated the League by several seasons. The first cup final was played in 1872, the Wanderers defeating the Royal Engineers. Of the 15 entries 13 were from the south, the others being Donington School and Queen's Park (Glasgow). Queen's Park was excused from playing until the semi-final round as a reward for its willingness to travel south, but frustration followed for it drew its match with the Wanderers and then was obliged to return home before the replay for lack of funds. The Cup continued to be won by gentlemanly southern sides until 1883–4 when it was won by Blackburn Rovers who had turned professional in 1880, having originated as the Blackburn Grammar School Old Boys. Blackburn Rovers won again the following year and, in both finals, beat Queen's Park, the second of those two years being the last to see an amateur side in the final.

Queen's Park, formed in 1867, continued as an amateur club for over 100 years and was still playing as such in the second division of the Scottish Football League in 1975. Early on it frequently won the Scottish FA Cup and last appeared in the final in 1900. There were many amateur clubs in Scotland at this period, but Scotland still achieved remarkable success in international matches in spite of exporting many of their best players to England to become professionals. England first played Scotland at football in 1872, Wales in 1879, and Ireland in 1882. The Football League did not start until 1888. It was immediately very popular and four years later had two divisions. The Scottish League started in 1890.

The public was not so interested in Rugby football. It was a players' game and not a spectacle. Because of it and because the 'natural' game had been to kick and not to handle it, it remained rigidly amateur, controlled by those who had learnt the game at school. It was well organized nonetheless. England played Scotland for the first time in the season 1870–1, Ireland in 1874–5, Wales in 1880–1, and France in 1905–6. Oxford first played Cambridge in 1871–2.

But before the turn of the century the great schism occurred in the Rugby game. This happened in the 1890s when the players of Yorkshire left the gentlemen of the south. The schism produced another good game, the professional Rugby League, exciting and tough and much to the taste of Yorkshire and Lancashire crowds. The schism came about because the workers of the northern clubs were finding it difficult to play in away matches without losing wages and endangering their employment by having time off. They wanted 'broken time' money and when the vote went against them, 22 clubs left the Association. In 1893 the Association had had 481 member clubs; by 1903 membership was reduced to 244.

The three games of football developed and codified during this period meant that large numbers of young men living under urban or semi-urban conditions now had a satisfactory outlet for aggression and competitive instincts. * Their elders, too old to play but with emotion to expend, could watch, shout, and gain armchair satisfaction from talking over the day's play and the positions of their favourite teams in the league tables. Nothing at this time was more important than the provision made by society, including an embryo entertainment industry, for spectator sport.

To Major Walter C. Wingfield went the unusual honour of inventing what was to become a new major sport. This was lawn tennis, which he had not intended to be new, only a more popular form of tennis. However, apart from the striking of a ball across a net with a racket there proved to be small resemblance between the two games. Wingfield's court was wider at the baselines than at the net and was often referred to as having the shape of an hour-glass. It was a portable court, to be set up indoors or out and it was given the inappropriate name of sphairistike. A patent was applied for in 1874, a unique occurence in itself, and the first championship was held at the

---

*Talking on the subject of games and aggression in 1974, a parson said: 'The worst year of my life was the year I gave up playing rugger. I had no idea, until I stopped playing, how much that weekly work-out in the scrum had meant to me.'

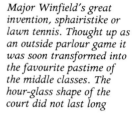

*Major Winfield's great
invention, sphairistike or
lawn tennis. Thought up as
an outside parlour game it
was soon transformed into
the favourite pastime of
the middle classes. The
hour-glass shape of the
court did not last long*

All England Lawn Tennis Club in 1877, men's singles only. It was a fortuitous event for the former All England Croquet Club at Wimbledon, which, three years earlier when short of funds, had added courts of the new game to help its finances. Doubles were included in 1879, ladies' singles in 1884, ladies' and mixed doubles in 1913. The game had been accepted as suitable for ladies from its invention, looked on as it was at first as a superior kind of parlour game, in harmony with long-skirted, unathletic play. It performed this function so well that for fifty years the tennis party became the social summer corollary of the private dance, much approved of by match-making mammas who took as much trouble over arranging partners as they did over the seat plan at dinners. And for the majority of daughters, who did not aspire to excellence or even competence at the game, they were quite right. They expected gentlemen to behave with consideration on the court, just as when out on their bicycles they expected them to mend their punctures. Long skirts, of course, disappeared after World War I (1919) when Mlle Lenglen began her leggy reign on the centre courts.

For the serious man player lawn tennis was never pat-ball and he was soon joined by a few serious ladies; such players had to be schizophrenic, or very much in love, to enjoy the tennis party. Years were to roll by before a man could safely serve fast to a lady, and in Letchworth, and probably elsewhere, when hard courts were added to the amenities of a club in the inter-war years, the men managed to pass a rule that only men should play on them, the ladies being confined to grass. Those women who did play seriously did so from the baseline and, from the 1880s onwards, they were assisted in their endeavours by a quickening of enthusiasm for physical education, several colleges for women being founded in the following thirty years.

One sporting name, apart from that of W. G. Grace, was known to almost everybody at the turn of the century. That was C. B. Fry. A man of his age, devoted to sport, and interested above all in seeing that every man, woman and child got some opportunity to play, he edited a magazine for George Newnes (1904) named after himself, *C. B. Fry's Magazine of Sports and Outdoor Life*. The opening numbers were a social document of some importance. They summed up in their contents the 'public school' attitude of the time towards play as a moral force, and they showed that Fry was supported in his interpretation of the view by countless others. He could be called the Baden-Powell of the sports scene, and he enlisted the recreational interests of public men, sometimes without justification, in support of his enthusiastically held beliefs. Thus, in a series of character sketches accompanied by coloured portraits and entitled 'Outdoor Men', the first to be featured was the then Colonial Secretary, Mr Alfred Lyttelton, an England player of cricket and football, and virtuous, according to the article, in all the nicer ways. Lyttelton, the article said, looked forward to the day when every hamlet would have its Saturday cricket match and it continued: 'Mr. Lyttelton preaches the gospel of this magazine. It is what sport means, what it is worth to a man's character, that matters; it is the spiritual significance, not the place in the averages that really counts.' After that it was not surprising to find the second article in the series devoted to Arthur Winnington-Ingram, Bishop of London (whose special interest was lawn tennis). He was followed by Lord Hawke (cricket), Admiral Sir John Fisher (Royal Navy and dancing), Field Marshal Earl Roberts (all-rounder), and most surprising of all, since he appeared far from enthusiastic, Sir Oliver Lodge (occasional golf). Each article was a sermon. Another parallel series 'Out of Harness' ran short pieces on current favourites of the news, several at a time, listing their recreational habits. Among those included were the Prime Minister, Arthur Balfour, good at a number of games; Sarah Bernhardt, 'up early, between five and six'; and the German Crown Prince (Little Willy to those who remember), 'not an ardent military man', who often left his studies in favour of lawn tennis.

Not quite everyone agreed with the text of the day *mens sana in corpore sano*. Mr Gladstone himself had been horrified by Sir Edward Grey's addiction, as he thought, to fly-fishing. But most people wearing the right ties did conform to this philosophy or, at least, made an excellent appearance of conforming. The kinds of play advocated were public school games, team games which taught the players to strive for their side, to take knocks and to improve their physique, all assets for the future in the game of life. Fry did not omit the ladies. He showed them at tennis, badminton and golf and he showed them, in gym slips, being coached for cricket. And one conviction of later generations about Edwardian England can be seen to be wrong—the sun did not always shine. An early number contained a photograph taken at the Oval cricket ground showing a bag of sawdust and a besom in the foreground. Apparently taken in 1903, the caption read: 'Last Year!'

Most of the men who supported the organization of games for competitive play were products of the public schools. The official recognition of games had come as long ago as 1864 when the Public School Commission reported to Parliament. It had applauded the introduction of games into the curriculum, for games were 'creators of health' and formers of 'some of the most valuable social qualities and manly virtues'. The only caveat was: 'The importance which the boys themselves attach to games is somewhat greater than might reasonably be desired, but within limits it is highly useful.' By about 1890 the same commissioners would probably have thought that those limits had been reached and passed, for by then there was a generation of masters worshipping games and assuming that only athletic boys could exercise authority successfully within a school. A. C. Benson, who had taught for twenty years at Eton before going to Cambridge as a don, reflected sadly that schools were now failing to develop intellectual abilities. He did not refer to 'flannelled fools at the wicket or the muddied oafs at the goals' as Kipling did, but he did write: 'They play games ardently, and fill their hours of leisure with talk about them. Yet one discerns in mind after mind the germs of intellectual things, undeveloped and bewildered.'

Perhaps the last word on this subject should be left to an article entitled 'Swimming for the Million' in *The Gentleman's Magazine* of October 1870.

In these days, when athletic sports of almost all kinds are in the ascendant, when the culture of the body is looked upon as of equal importance to that of the mind, and the 'muscular' divides the favour of, at least, the *cognoscenti* with the Ritualistic form of Christianity, there surely needs no long argument based upon mere physiological grounds to recommend for more general use an exercise [swimming] which possesses the double advantage of developing the forces of the muscles, whilst it contributes largely to strengthen those of the nervous system, and, through it, the operations of the mind.

The reason for this is not far to seek. The nature of the employment of a large majority of an urban population now-a-days is such as to dwarf and diminish the muscular, whilst it develops and excites the nervous element of the body. The race after wealth, which keeps an ever-increasing number of the ambitious in a turmoil of alternate hope and despair; the competition for the means of living which pervades the great middle-class, and the rage for excitement and sensuous pleasure which finds employment for a large part of those who are blessed, or cursed, as it may be, with abundant means and leisure, all these tend to produce an irritable and unstable condition of the nerve element, that element which ought to regulate and harmonize all the operations of the system, from the digestion and assimilation of the food, up to the highest operations of the mind. These are the classes, our overworked artizans, shopkeepers, and busy men of commerce, pent up, as they are for the most part, in close and ill ventilated rooms for many hours a day, whose frames require the stimulus afforded by the impact of fresh air and cold water. Their lungs, oppressed with the dust and mustiness of close rooms, crave for the stimulus of the country breezes, and their relaxed skins for the friction of the soft but exciting touch of the crystal wave.

*Sandpits for children not often at the seaside were a welcome if primitive
innovation*

It was not only the gentlemen who were busy about physical recreation.
The town authorities were also showing their keenness: the Lincoln City
Commons Act (1871), for example, stated that it would be 'greatly for the
benefit of the inhabitants of the city if part of the Monks Leys Common were
converted into a public park or pleasure ground'. In sympathy with
Victorian ideas the park was named the *Arboretum* and constructed with
pleasant walks through lawns and leafy glades. There were many flowerbeds
and a fashionable glasshouse. Hundreds of similar parks had been created or
were soon to be created throughout the country. Recreation areas for cricket,
football, lawn tennis and bowls followed quickly. Lincoln, like other towns,
had promoted a private bill in 1871 to get powers to act, but after 1875 the
Public Health Act covered local authorities wishing to continue the good
work, and amendment acts enabled them to charge admission for particular
areas on so many days in the year, including marking off an area of pond for
skating. There was a Parks Regulation Act (1872) which gave park-keepers,
within the park, the powers of police constables to see that regulations about
hours of opening, lighting fires, climbing trees, playing games and dressing
decently were kept. The Commons Act of 1899 transferred the control of
these open spaces from churchwardens and overseers to the new councils.
Once the way had been shown there was seemingly no end to it. Before long
the bigger local authorities were providing gymnasia, swimming baths, rifle
ranges, boating opportunities, dramatic entertainments, bands in the parks,
refreshments, concerts, dance halls, piers, holiday camps, and indeed almost
anything in the recreational line that could justify public expenditure.

143

There was a corollary to the growth of towns and the determination to provide local facilities for play; this was the growth of imperialism and the assumption that where the flag went it was accompanied by British play. The sun, which at that time was popularly supposed to be kept busy not setting on the British Empire, was also required the year round for cricket. The enthusiasm for cricket throughout the empire was one of the strangest phenomena of sporting history. Apart from a certain status it enjoyed in Holland, cricket had never appealed much to the foreigner. Nevertheless, wherever the flag went for colonization and trade, cricket went with it. It did not survive in the USA but elsewhere it became a delirium. Tours before 1914 were all to countries populated by large numbers of men and women of British descent; it was not believed at that time that Indians, Pakistanis or West Indians would ever be able to play the other cricketing countries on level terms. The first English tour in Australia was in 1876–7; the first Australian tour in England, 1880. Between 1876 and 1914 England had been in Australia nineteen times, and Australia in England seventeen times. South Africa came to England twice before 1914 and England went to South Africa seven times. There were also a few matches between South Africa and Australia.

In other sports and games before 1914 only matches between England, Scotland, Wales and Ireland created the illusion of regular international play, but everywhere the seeds were being sown in spite of the difficulties of travelling, particularly that of time. France joined in the cross-country championships and came second in 1908; boxing was thoroughly international but not as a team sport; golf, at which the Americans were already excelling, was in the same category. At football England played Austria several times before 1914, occasionally other teams, and there were three matches against South Africa. At Rugby football the home countries played some matches against France, all of them in this century. The Davis Cup competition for lawn tennis was started in 1900, all the winners before 1914 being from the United States, the British Isles and Australasia. At rowing the first foreign crew to win the Grand Challenge Cup at Henley came from Belgium in 1906, although a Dutch crew had won the Thames Challenge Cup in 1895. A Canadian crew won the Stewards' Challenge Cup for four oars in 1910. Yachting had become the rich man's sport and there had been international competition for a great many years; his other exclusive play, polo, had enjoyed Westchester Cup international matches between England and the United States since 1866. The British also got much polo in India, playing Indian Princes' teams.

Behind the growth of international sport, and giving it impetus, were the revived Olympic Games. The original Games had been held at four-year intervals for a thousand years from 776 BC. Baron Pierre de Coubertin, a Frenchman and the instigator of the revival, was convinced that the greatness of Ancient Greece had rested at least to some extent on its insistence that physical perfection was one ingredient of civilization. No announcement could have been more to the liking of the majority at the end of the nineteenth century. De Coubertin held a meeting at the Sorbonne in 1894 and at it nine countries were represented. As a result the first of the new Olympic Games were held at Athens in 1896, when athletes of thirteen

(above) Photography was not everybody's hobby yet, but you could have your
likeness taken

(below) The donkey ride was not confined to the seaside. This one could be taken
in London

nations took part. Most of the events were athletics, including the marathon, but there was some swimming, cycling, fencing, gymnastics and shooting. Four more games were held before 1914, when war put a temporary stop to the sequence. They were held in Paris in 1900, St Louis in 1904, London in 1908 and Stockholm in 1912. Twenty-eight nations sent competitors to the 1912 games.

On the other side of the Atlantic sport was as dominating as in England. Baseball was the summer game, ousting cricket but failing to impress other countries. Baseball originated in 1839 in a village in New York State. As was usual there was some obscurity about the matter, so in 1908 a distinguished group of men associated with the game were appointed privately as a commission to investigate it. They found that the game owed nothing to rounders, or any other foreign game, and declared that the first rules were the invention of Abner Doubleday. However not everyone felt happy about this pronouncement, so puzzlingly at variance with commonsense, and eventually it was refuted by various independent investigators. These showed that baseball was a well-known word in England in the eighteenth century, and produced with the evidence was a child's book, *A Little Pretty Pocket-Book* (England 1744), with 'B is for Baseball' and an accompanying illustration showing a player at the plate. Nevertheless the argument went on.

The United States had another game, peculiar to itself, American football. As in the British Isles so in the States there were many kinds of football being played up to the 1870s. In the Princeton rules of 1867, twenty-five players formed a team. An intercollegiate match was played in 1869 between Princeton and Rutgers with twenty-five players on each side. As in England again, it was the educational establishments that created the variety in football and when Harvard, favouring a running game, played McGill University of Montreal for lack of opponents nearer home, the way had been opened for a special brand of football to evolve.

The oldest organized game in North America was lacrosse. It had been played by the Iroquois Indians as a war game for years before America was rediscovered and it was known to them as 'baggataway'; lacrosse was the French Canadian name, given because the stick with its net resembled a crozier. Several times in recent decades lacrosse has seemed likely to become a really popular game but it has never quite managed it. In the United States it was played chiefly in schools and colleges; Canadians were more enthusiastic; and in England it had a large following in the north. The women's game, less violent and prettier to watch, started around 1900; its firmest hold in England and the USA was between the wars.

Another game, often thought of as American or Canadian because of the money spent in those countries building special rinks, was ice-hockey. In fact Holland and other European countries had played games resembling ice-hockey for centuries, and before 1914 a European championship had been started. There were outstandingly good teams in the US and Canada in those days but their appearance overseas had to wait until the 1920s when the World Cup was started. It was the same with other ice events, although there was a great increase in popularity following the invention of the

The oratorio and concerts of all kinds were well attended. There was music in the home, in the church halls and the drawing rooms, everywhere in fact

'Glaciarium', the first refrigerated rink built in London in 1876.

Roller skating was a craze in the United States in the 1860s. It was popular in England but the way it swept America was phenomenal. It began with society on the Eastern seaboard and then, gathering momentum as it crossed the country, it erupted in Chicago where a vast arena was built to accommodate 1000 skaters and 3000 spectators. In popular clamour the enthusiasm for play in the United States surpassed anything known in England. The whole country was wild about it and if Bostonians looked down their noses in disapproval at the way the new society was mingling, the rest of the United States did not care. As for society in England, it watched and shuddered at the American ability to turn such pastimes as archery, croquet, and Highland games into a frenzy of uninhibited enjoyment and noise.

Another amusement that England and America shared at this time was the theatre. Not quite so readily as now but still readily enough, actors and actresses crossed the ocean when required. The theatre's lean period in both countries was over, and with Henry Irving at the Lyceum, London, under the management of H. L. Bateman, an American, prospects had greatly improved. The first big success was *The Bells* and this was followed by a number of Shakespearean productions, not all to the public's enthusiastic taste but, in sum, for Irving a personal triumph. With Ellen Terry as his leading lady his appeal to the middle classes was tremendous. But England and the States now had another stage delight, the Gilbert and Sullivan operas, beginning with *Trial by Jury* in 1875. It was still a melodramatic age but beginning to enjoy naughtiness and wit. More wit was supplied by Oscar

The summer season in London and elsewhere brought the garden party and with it another opportunity to look one's best

Wilde and some of the naughtiness, but in the years immediately preceding World War I the music hall brought the greatest pleasure to the greatest number. It was peculiarly English, bawdy, sentimental, pretty and tuneful, as unsophisticated as it could be; it pleased the audience, they sang songs and it went well with the beer, the national drink.

Culture was in the concert halls. Orchestral instruments had greatly improved during the century and there was now much great music to play. Sir Henry Wood introduced the Promenade Concerts in 1895, there was fine church music for organ and choirs, good songs for amateurs were sold in abundance and the pianoforte scores of Chopin and Lizt were on the music rests of every aspiring daughter of suburban homes. The art galleries were also thriving. Britain had produced artists much to its own sentimental taste.

A street musi playing an instrument le convenient th the barrel org

They could not compare with the French impressionists but at that time few Englishmen responded to the work of those bewildering artists and much preferred the English scene, the draped female, horses, stags and dogs.

One London pleasure that lasted throughout these forty-four years was the Season. For the rich it was the time of year when it was practically compulsory to be in the capital, especially if they valued social life or had sons and daughters to marry off. For the poor of London, undisturbed by politics, it was the great, open-air, free spectacle of the year. There was an opportunity to watch the parades in the park, the comings and goings at social functions and the discomfiture of nobs and their servants when running the gauntlet of Cockney wit and comment. *The Gentleman's Magazine* for June 1870 set the scene: the town was inundated with visitors,

The polka was still riot, as shown in his earlier picture by Doyle

clubs were roused from lethargy, Italians made 'bright and sparkling music in Covent Garden', 'Belgravia became re-animated', and in the park 'the equipage of royalty rolls side by side with the carriage of the courtesan'.

All the same, and in spite of the big increase during the period of opportunities for play, time for amusing oneself was very limited for the bulk of the population. Hours of labour were long in the five and a half day working week and even the heathen kept his blinds drawn if he wished to indulge himself on Sunday. For Sunday, by convention, had become a workday: for not doing anything for fun, for repressing every inclination to use free time for pleasure and for pleasing God by being bored. That left Saturday afternoon and even today in the minds of many elderly people those few hours are synonymous with freedom.

13

Change was slower in the country; aping the townsman was not a rural pleasure. However some middle class people with little or no interest in hunting or other country pursuits were beginning to move out of the towns and into the countryside. Their sporting interest might be golf (first amateur championship, 1885; first ladies' championship, 1893) or, in the evenings, billiards (first amateur championship, 1888), a game that fitted in well with those who had work to do during the day, making homecoming rather late. The dreamlike quality of the really well-to-do's daily routine continued of course (Siegfried Sassoon's *Memoirs of a Fox-Hunting Man* was a perfect summary of one man's world that ended in 1914), and there was whist in the big houses as well as in the village halls. But more hostesses than ever before were presuming to arrange dances in the winter, musical evenings and cards; and, in the summer, lawn tennis parties, croquet parties, archery perhaps, and, if near a convenient river, boating picnics or picnics in woods. Picnics were in vogue; everyone enjoyed or pretended to enjoy them. Not that they were new—the Wordsworths adored them and celebrated victory at Waterloo with a vast picnic on the top of Skiddaw. On such occasions servants accompanied the picnickers but now everyone was at it, the cockney on Hampstead Heath and the *Three Men in a Boat*.

One of the remoter parts where in 1870 not much change had taken place was the Welsh borderland. The Reverend Francis Kilvert was a curate in Clyro above Hay on Wye in the seventies. His place in society was carefully defined; he was welcome everywhere, but not free to choose a wife from any household. Fortunately for posterity he was an accurate observer and recorder and his observations included play. In the summer his life was a kaleidoscope of archery and croquet, bazaars, flower shows and picnics. His winter was not so enviable. On rare occasions there was skating: 'I had the honour of being knocked down by Lord Royston'. Lady Royston, he observed, skated and took turns to be pulled about the ice in a sledge chair. A special part of the ice was marked off with a rope for 'sliders'. A quadrille band came from Malmesbury. Quadrilles and the Lancers were danced and, after dark, the ice was lit by Chinese lanterns. Skaters danced arm in arm holding torches in their hands. A fire balloon was sent up. All that was unusual excitement. More regular was shooting, but Kilvert did not shoot. An entry for Monday 13 November 1871 read: ' "What a fine day it is. Let us go out and kill something." The old reproach against the English. The squire has just gone by with a shooting party. A line of gentlemen walking first followed by keepers carrying the guns and a *posse comitatus* of beaters and

Not many ladies cared for the penny-farthing bicycle—it was too far to fall

boys and dogs and hangers on.' And another reference: 'four guns killed 700 rabbits in one afternoon'.

Kilvert did his best to help others but he recognized that the poor had few pleasures. The rows, the fights and men lying drunk by the roadside 'cursing, muttering, maundering and vomiting' worried him and he did not attend the Clyro Feast Ball but lay awake listening to the 'scraping and squealing of the fiddle and the ceaseless heavy tramp of the dancers'. He enjoyed nevertheless the football after the Whitney Harvest Festival and dinner with all the men. Penny readings gave him another opportunity of helping, for he took a great interest in them, and improved the entertainment by introducing songs and instrumental interludes.

In the much more sophisticated atmosphere of Cambridge another kind of life was recalled in retrospect by Gwen Raverat in *Period Piece*. Gwen's father was George Darwin, a son of Charles; her mother was Maud du Puy, an adventurous lady and an American. Gwen was born in 1885 all ready for the bicycle age. Gwen's mother had the first tricycle in Cambridge and, with Gwen on a small one, and Charles her brother standing on the back bar of his mother's they set off on expeditions. Father sometimes went too, on a new safety bicycle. Later on when they had bicycles with pneumatic tyres Mr and Mrs Darwin, wearing evening dress, cycled to dinner parties.

It would not be easy to overestimate the social importance of the bicycle between 1880 and 1914. It increased opportunities for play because it offered to thousands chances of freedom previously unknown. In consequence it was an object of unprecedented devotion. Just as George Darwin was always caring for his so, all over the country, ordinary men, women and children of every class were looking after theirs. It was a point of honour to look after it yourself. Men joined clubs and escaped on Sundays in knickerbocker suits

By 1895 ladies were making the best of new opportunities

*y fishing in a
m stream*

and matching caps, and women went for unchaperoned rides.* In spite of minor accidents, and the frustrations caused by chains coming off, there was something poetical about riding a bicycle. A Dean of Norwich, Henry Charles Beeching, expressed it in 'Going Down Hill on a Bicycle'.

> With lifted feet, hands still,
> I am poised, and down the hill
> Dart, with heedful mind;
>   The air goes by in the wind . . .
>
>   *   *   *
>
> Speed slackens now, I float
> Awhile in my airy boat;
> Till, when the wheels scarce crawl
> My feet to the treadles fall.

Lifted feet because then it was impossible to free-wheel, the pedals had to go round. They were soon going round even faster, for the World Championships were held in England in 1904, nearly forty years after Napoleon III had first offered a prize for a bicycle race; that was on a boneshaker (the velocipede), and was followed in England and then on the Continent by penny-farthing races and championships from 1878. The championships were continued on the safety bicycle after its introduction in 1885. They were all of interest to the public since they, too, were on wheels; but even more intriguing were the daring ladies who wore bloomers, calling loud attention to the unsuitability of women's sporting attire.

Nothing much else in the country was new, but men came out from the towns, often on their bicycles, to fish along the banks of the meandering rivers and canals. They sought escape from urban life and, although in competitions they were only yards from fellow competitors on the banks, they got it.

---

*The author's mother and father found bicycles invaluable for courting in 1903–4 in spite of his mother's huge hats which fashion required her to wear.

One regular entertainment that the whole country clung to was the fair. Whether it was a feast or the 'staty' (statute fair) it was an event planned for and looked forward to. Most of these fairs were now for pleasure only, although some kept their connection with trade. A picture of fairs, their importance and the life connected with them in the nineteenth century was left for posterity by Lord George Sanger in his *Seventy Years a Showman*. George's father went on the road with a peep-show, his first box being fitted with six peep-holes with strong lenses and 'moveable and very gaudy pictures' of the Battle of Trafalgar where he had fought and witnessed the death of Nelson. This simple entertainment depended for success partly on the patter accompanying the pictures and partly on being up to date. When William IV died George's father quickly manufactured scenes from the lying-in-state and the funeral. Favourites like *Maria Marten; or, The Murder in the Red Barn* were part of his stock-in-trade.

According to Sanger the first fair of the year in the south was at Reading on May Day, the showmen leaving their winter quarters to attend it; it lasted one day, then on to Henley for 3 May. At this early date (1833) the big names of the show world were Wombwell, Nelson Lee, Hilton, Randall and Taylor. Wombwell's and Hilton's were rivals in menageries and each had more than one 'collection' on the road. Freaks, true and false, were very popular and these, with the peep-shows, were sandwiched between the big men at the great fair in Hyde Park to celebrate Queen Victoria's coronation in 1838. The giants of the profession had circuses, waxworks, theatres, marionettes and menageries. Richardson's theatre was famous and Richardson's also owned the City of London theatre in Shoreditch.

By this time Sanger's peep-show had twenty-four peep-holes and he operated also a hand-turned roundabout, the hands being those of local boys in exchange for free rides. When George added to his contribution it was with performing mice, hen canaries and two redpolls. He took £9 at Cowes, a huge sum. More important, he married into the profession, choosing a celebrity, Madame Pauline de Vere, the Lady of the Lions; Queen Victoria had been sorry for her because she looked pale when she put her head into the lion's mouth. George was an elaborately dressed conjuror at some fairs when he included 'a hanky-panky second sight and thought reading business' with a sister-in-law. Families stuck together.

By 1871, the beginning of the period under review, George had progressed so well that he took over Astley's Amphitheatre with its menagerie. Astley, in Sanger's words, 'was the historical English home of the riders of the ring' for its name had been famous for one hundred years. Sanger was England's Barnum, whose reign in the United States had been even more colourful; Sanger boasted that he was a match for any competition, including Buffalo Bill.

George Sanger made two points about the change in social attitudes during his long showman's life. The first was the steady decline in superstition for, when he first went on the road, it had been far easier to mystify country people and to trade on their fears. He had also been refused permission to conjure in Scotland and had been warned from appearing in York. His second point, ironic because he met a violent death, was the general

Come to the fair, more modern style and come they did in great numbers in towns

improvement in behaviour, it being no longer necessary to make provision for protecting the show against local roughs. There was still plenty of drinking and fighting in 1914 but society was learning fast to deplore excess and to appreciate the many other outlets for fun available to all.

But still the love of slaughtering animals went on. The rich, if adventurous, now turned their attention to Africa and India for big game hunting and shooting. It was to be a short-lived sport since for every man who shot for enjoyment there was another, at least, who was doing it for gain. As a sport, because of the danger, the appeal was very strong, as any volume of *The Badminton Magazine of Sports and Pastimes* proves. That of January–June 1897, for example, contained ten substantial articles on big game shooting and hunting and, if fishing is included, three-quarters of each monthly part was devoted to the killing of something. The other quarter consisted of articles on a catholic selection of pursuits that a gentleman might patronize: cricket, golf, cycling and, in season, tobogganing. *The Field* (founded 1853), inspired by Surtees, was wider in its appeal but neither it, nor the magazines devoted to stories for men and boys, could afford to ignore the emotional response there always was to narratives about big game hunts.

The number of books on games and sports being published was considerable, particularly if books on natural history are included. Dozens of authors and publishers worked to satisfy the demand. There were also a quantity of books, expensive and cheap, on social play, particularly for women: how to amuse oneself at home, how to comport oneself at dances and in public places, how to dress appropriately for every occasion, how to improve one's looks and health ('most women change their underclothing far too seldom') and how to arrange a dinner table for a party. Women were more than ready, judging by sales, to accept advice from, and to read a book written for them by, a Lady. *Etiquette for Women* by One of the Aristocracy, published by C. Arthur Pearson in their Popular Shilling Books, was one best-seller. Every girl then, including those below stairs, wanted to be a lady although it was not long, with the arrival of the silent screen, before she was seeing herself as Alma Taylor or Chrissy White.

Even the small circus usually had a lion or two and a trainer who must be obeyed

14

☆ *BETWEEN THE WARS 1919–1939* ☆

When the war of 1914–18 ended, with its unparalleled slaughter of the ordinary man in the humiliating conditions of trench warfare, there were two spirits abroad; one was to build a country fit for heroes (and the general physical standard of the poorer classes at recruitment was relevant here), and the other was to get back to the good old days, to live and forget. Neither purpose was achieved. The gaiety of the smart set in the twenties gave way to anxiety and more serious attitudes following the great depression, unemployment and the rise of Hitler in Nazi Germany, and coincided with a strong pacifist movement which had some noble support.

Those who were young at the time could bear testimony to England's quick return after World War I to the two-nation mentality. The rich tried to revive their world of gentlemen and players, with lavish parties and presentations at court, the remnants of a Season and the kind of mirage world outlined by Beverley Nichols in *The Sweet and Twenties*. The young went wild, out to shock, particularly the ladies with their elongated figures created by their clothes. They flung themselves about the streets in 'open' cars, enjoyed the noisiest parties and outraged the serious ballroom dancers with the charleston. It was a throwback to the early nineteenth century when bucks went on sprees, only this time the ladies went with them. Even

ing the
eston in the
. Everyone
oing it

the General Strike (1926) was accepted as an adorable opportunity for the gigantic play of driving trains and buses. It was not altogether surprising; many had a lot to forget, and fled from the mental pictures that haunted their hours alone.

At the public schools the mood of the twenties was in favour of recapturing all the standards of the years before the war. Games were returned to their pedestal. As late as 1929, Cyril Norwood, Headmaster of Harrow School, included in his book *The English Tradition of Education*—he called it 'a statement of faith and hope'—a chapter on athletics, extolling their virtues. He meant by athletics 'that which not only produces, and promotes bodily fitness, but also through the training of the body develops the right type of character'. He regarded the inspiration of athletics to have

The crowded ballrooms of the twenties were to be found everywhere. This one was on the Criterion Roof Garden

It was, is, fashionable to be at Eton on the Fourth of June

come from 'usages of chivalry', and its invaluable contribution to be that of moulding character through teams. He did not approve of the more individual games at school, and he gave pride of place to Rugby football. So did other people. Robert Collis, a Rugbeian and an Irish international, described the feeling when awarded his Cambridge blue: 'In England the gaining of a "blue" is generally regarded as a more desirable achievement than becoming an M.P., or being made a knight. The social position it confers lasts for many years, for to be an "old blue" is to have an assured status for the rest of life.' *

*From *The Silver Fleece*.

Collis's autobiography was published in 1936 and his views, which were the same as the author's at this time, were already beginning to be out of date. As early as 1932 L. B. Pekin wrote *Public Schools: Their Failure and Reform* (admittedly it was published by Leonard and Virginia Woolf at the Hogarth Press), in which he tried to give games the importance he thought they deserved. He argued strongly that a much wider range of options should be open to boys instead of 'days wasted by interminable games of fourth-rate cricket'. Changes were slow but inevitable: T. C. Worsley recalled in *Flannelled Fool* (1967) that some of his ideas were countenanced because he was 'capable of making a hundred against the school'.

The play of the workaday majority, if they played at all, was not much changed. In the south there were more leagues, more facilities for play on recreation grounds and in local authority parks, but play for most was a Saturday afternoon affair, with practically nothing on Sunday. The richer club player enjoyed Sunday tennis, cricket and golf on private grounds. Up north, life could be dreary, for unemployment made many areas a different world from the commercial and relatively prosperous south-east. Even there, however, village, works and town teams managed Saturday afternoon and evening play. Bowls was strong and darts in pubs became a major occupation for a host of players.

Too many did not play at all except by association, standing in the wind on rain-swept terraces or on the field, or alternatively following the racing and the boxing news in the then numerous special editions of the evening papers. It was seedy, comfortless and disheartening. The hopeful spirit of the first decade of the century and the elation after the end of the war in 1918 were dead and in their place was despair or cynicism. Attendances at football matches were enormous: 60,000 was the expectation on the most important grounds, and in some areas the Saturday game seemed just the only extra worth living for. There was *one* other thing: the football pools, 'more conspicuous in Liverpool than anywhere else' said a famous report made to the Pilgrim Trust, *Men Without Work* (1938).

> It is the all-pervading atmosphere of football pools, greyhounds and horses. This has become such an important environmental factor that, for the individual unemployed, it is an effort to develop interests unconnected with them. The extent to which the interests and indeed the whole lives of so many Liverpool unemployed centre round the pools must be seen to be believed. The queues at Post Offices filling in coupons, the number of 'guaranteed systems' for correct forecasting on sale in Liverpool's poorest districts, the periodicals containing nothing but pool analyses, the dirty and torn sports columns of the papers in Public Libraries . . . It is not a direct interest in sport, but it derives from that and gives glamour to everything and everybody that has anything to do with sport. On a Saturday afternoon, when an important League match is on, the unemployed men in Liverpool turn out and gather along the streets where the crowds go up by foot, tram, bus or motor car to watch it. To watch a match is in itself a second-hand experience, and the unemployed man, not often able to afford a shilling for entrance, has to make do with this substitute for it. And he seems to derive excitement of a kind even from this. But there is a world of difference between this and Tonypandy people turning out to the last man to welcome Tommy Farr [the boxer] with flags and posters and civic honours.

The dogs. Greyhound racing had a great appeal between the wars and still draws crowds

There was little aggression on the terraces then for the physique of those who might have been aggressive was poor and, in any case, the war for the time being had diminished man's desire to fight and provoke.

'The dogs' were another phenomenon of the twenties. They were a natural in the north where coursing had never lost its popularity and to own a dog (ie a greyhound) was many men's ambition. Attempts to arrange meetings where greyhounds pursued imitation hares had been known earlier in the century but 1919 saw the first track opened, in the United States. Its success was not unheeded in England where the Belle Vue, Manchester, track was ready for meetings in 1926. The times were unpropitious but still large crowds gathered and, after argument, totalizators were installed to assist betting as they had been on horse racecourses earlier. Horse racing continued to draw crowds and the name of Gordon Richards, the jockey, was a household one.

Life in the country during the twenties was generally better. Wages were low but there were no concentrations of unemployment and opportunities for play were all around. Apart from cricket and football there were often rivers for fishing, boating and bathing (pollution was seldom mentioned, only an occasional word of warning not to bathe in a particular area). Those who could afford to holiday at popular seaside resorts found themselves back at the fair on a more lavish scale than Thurston's was able to bring round. It was still the exception rather than the rule to go on holiday, apart from day

161

trips or during wakes' weeks for those in employment in some northern towns. The crowded conditions of south-west seaside villages and the boom in holiday camps were then unknown; only rich people and students went abroad and a feature of the home market, for a wide range of the middle classes, were the huge holiday haunts publications (over 1000 pages) of the railways. These contained thousands of small advertisements, often with accompanying photographs, of suitable boarding and lodging houses.

Looking back, the two nations seemed well divided, especially in summer, between the white-trousered, be-blazered gentlemen of the south and the shapeless suited, cloth-capped, undernourished players of the north. The comparison is too neat to be truthful, but in sport, as socially in everything else, the two nations were still accepted as natural divisions. The fact that this order was constantly being contested, not only politically but educationally through more grammar school scholarships and further scholarships to universities, was pushed on one side. Clubs felt the irritation of it. There was a decline in the social exclusiveness of field sports and in all games club committees pondered deeply over applications for membership which came from good players whose social background left something to be desired. Lawn tennis clubs, because they were mixed, provided the biggest dilemmas in provincial towns. Daughters' partners should be of the marriageable sort.

Certain social games, or games that had become social, were now personal options without popular following. Archery, no longer in demand as a vehicle for male attentions to the female, was one of them; so was croquet, too good a game to be forgotten. Socially their place had been taken by auction bridge, a passion in the thirties for players of all ages but not of all classes, some still preferring whist. Dancing was a universal pleasure. Tea dances were common in restaurants, big towns had the 'palais' and small ones their church halls or other rooms. New freedoms for young men and women led to a growth in youth hostels and holiday fellowship camps and hostels. There was more general interest in walking, bicycling and climbing.

It was a satisfying period for the football gladiator, not so good for the cricketer. There was plenty of interest in cricket and crowds went to the test matches between England and Australia, but the county matches were ill-supported in spite of the keenness to read about them in the newspapers. One tremendous sensation was the body-line controversy which broke out in Australia during the England tour of 1932–3. * To the regular test-playing countries of Australia, England and South Africa were now added New Zealand, the West Indies (under white captains in spite of Constantine) and India (under Indians who were aristocrats). They were not then as good as they later became, but they added greatly to the pleasure of the international scene. Club cricket was in its best period. There was little difficulty in raising teams and southern business houses were willing to release players mid-week. The motor car helped a great deal and some performers, to their great

---

*The author at this period was working in the office of *The Cricketer* run by A. W. T. Langford and edited by P. F. Warner. 'Plum' was very emotional about body-line, loyally defending the English team in public and privately believing that D. R. Jardine, the English captain, and H. Larwood, the England fast bowler, were killing cricket.

(above) There was more opportunity to play after World War I but for a time clothes remained modestly old fashioned

(below) At the seaside or on the front in the twenties. Plenty to look at and time for a good sit

The Olympic Games of 1928 at Amsterdam. A fine piece of organization

pleasure, were regular members of touring sides because they owned one.

International play in other games also increased. It was not yet the aircraft age in spite of regular services between European countries but the world already felt smaller than in 1914. The Olympic Games began again, golfers of the USA were regularly winning British championships, lawn tennis players began their peripatetic habits and drivers of motor cars and riders of motor cycles did the same. On the whole it was individuals who did the travelling, except on very special occasions, for it was a big effort for a team to travel abroad and a bigger one still to include supporters.

As far as sport was concerned the thirties were the heyday for the newspapers. Columns of print were devoted daily to covering events of all kinds. A gentleman reading his *Times* or *Morning Post* could expect to find in-season reports of yesterday's individual hunts or an account of each county cricket match. Three or four of the cricket matches would be covered by special reporters, the sports agencies covering the rest. The *Manchester Guardian* and the *Daily Telegraph*, likewise, devoted several pages to sports. The *Manchester Guardian*, like *The Times*, would carry the best part of a column on an important tennis (real) or rackets match and the *Morning Post*, in an attempt to boost sales, published weekly articles on London club matches of major games with short reports on Bath Club Cup matches at squash rackets. Oxford and Cambridge and the public schools also got their weekly share of space. The BBC followed suit. They had little time to offer for minor sports but eye-witness accounts were a feature of a late-evening news bulletin, radio of course.

It was a time for heroes. All major games had them and nearly everybody talked about them. The cricketers were at least as numerous as the footballers. Hobbs and Sandham, Holmes and Sutcliffe, Hendren, Verity, Larwood, Bradman, Hammond were well enough known for their names to appear on the regular daily newspaper placards, and there were dozens more. W. W. Wakefield summed up all that was best in Rugby football while 'Boy' Bastin of Arsenal, Charles Buchan of the same club, Stan Cullis of Wolverhampton, Dixie Dean of Everton, to name only four out of the first four letters of the alphabet, were familiar to thousands who had never seen a first division football match. The boxers, Carpentier, Jack Dempsey and Tommy Farr; the tennis players, Fred Perry, 'Bunny' Austin and the Americans; the billiard players, J. Davis, W. Lindrum and T. Newman; the athletes, H. M. Abrahams, Lord Burleigh, J. E. Lovelock and J. Owens; the golfers, Bobby Jones and Henry Cotton; all of them enjoyed publicity which equalled that of film stars and all were aware of their importance in society,

The thirties were the great days of spectator sports and sporting heroes. Everyone knew the England opening bats, Hobbs and Sutcliffe. On good days they rated the evening newspapers' placards

*Women played cricket and other team games
with enthusiasm in the thirties*

*Mitcham ladies on a training run for the
coming athletics season in 1930*

especially to those whose lives were drab and lacking the colour which their heroes shed.

It was an unique period, too, for women's cricket, tennis (apart from tournament players), hockey and lacrosse. Women needed games after the war to emphasize the freedom it had given them and they took to them an enthusiasm that they have now lost. With them, as with men, it was the team games that counted and the standards reached were high. Individuals also did well. Joyce Wethered and Enid Wilson were among the best-known golfers, Mlle Lenglen, Helen Wills, and Dorothy Round were stars at tennis.

Smaller games like fives, tennis (real) and rackets were now better organized and did well particularly with their schools' competitions. It was the period of the old school tie and nearly everyone in the south who was entitled to do so flaunted some kind of colour or other. Nothing, in minor sport, quite equalled the sudden dedication to squash rackets, partly because the new purpose-built clubs were cosy with bars of their own and men and women members, and partly because it was a keep-fit age and squash a game that could be enjoyed at almost any level and well into middle age. Badminton also prospered, although the size of court demanded a gymnasium or church hall, reducing the comfort of the evening but not the enjoyment of the play.

The theatre enjoyed a popular period with many touring companies visiting the medium-sized towns. On the whole it was light-hearted, tuneful and sentimental. Bright comedies, like those of Lonsdale, featuring Gladys Cooper, Gerald du Maurier and Marie Lohr, and musical comedies, including *No! No! Nanette!* and *Rose Marie* and the very light operas *Lilac Time* and *Show Boat* (introducing Paul Robeson) were the diet of the twenties. By the thirties theatre-goers were ready for the sharper wit of Noel Coward's plays and the sentiment and gaiety of his musicals. On the continent the experimental theatre was flourishing but English audiences had little interest in it, except for J. B. Priestley's excursions into time and an occasional peep at Ernst Toller and Bertolt Brecht. There were nevertheless some fine actors and actresses, many of them appearing in memorable Shakespearean productions at the Old Vic or in the Open Air Theatre at Regent's Park. Shaw was still writing, T. S. Eliot had a following in poetry and D. H. Lawrence, in prose, was causing a stir. These were not the popular writers but between them and those who sold in millions (eg Ethel M. Dell) there were good novelists whose work occasionally had a wide appeal.

The universal attraction was the cinema: in the twenties the silent films with captions, and an orchestra or just one pianoforte interpreting emotions through the tunes they played; in the thirties, the talkies. Films and film stars lulled the critical faculties, so great was the novelty, and pictures that as books would never have achieved the distinction of being noticed were treated to long reviews. As an art form it was a minority interest but as the provider of romance (Rudolf Valentino), adventure (Douglas Fairbanks) and westerns (Tom Mix) the cinema created addicts who 'went to the pictures' two, three or more times a week. For the discharge of emotions, while holding hands in the dark, there had never been anything like it. There was also a real artist, Charlie Chaplin, and Mickey Mouse.

The small open car, the luggage on the grid and
cloche hats were all part of the play in the 1920s

Punts on the river in great numbers were a
feature of the 1930s' summers

Meanwhile the wireless—television started in 1938—was helping thousands to use their imagination in listening to stories and plays. It also had a triumph in its handling of music and in the creation of a Children's Hour which instructed and amused millions of those for whom it was intended and adults. Those were great days also for the gramophone which brought symphonies and famous orchestras into thousands of homes, as well as 'pop' music and jazz. It was also the era of the big dance bands, which alternated playing for dancing with concert performances of a spectacular kind. Simultaneously, mostly in the north, the brass bands continued making the kind of music that stirred the blood and touched the heart strings. Only the minor orchestral players were out of work, displaced by the talkies and the new interval entertainer, the cinema organ.

15

☆ *FUN FOR ALL 1945–1975* ☆

Except for a determined, nostalgic few there was no looking back after 1945. For better for worse, for richer for poorer, it was a different world and in no way, once the years of adjustment were over, was it to be more different than in play. There were to be no gentlemen and players, only people, and the play that they wanted was not team games—although they were still good spectacles if played excitingly enough—but doing one's own thing. Thousands, whose parents had not looked beyond Southend or Blackpool for their holidays, now hitch-hiked, male and female together, across Europe; others took coach trips and visited in time the capital cities and beauty spots of a continent. Italy and Spain were crowded with tourists, as was Britain in return; a growing number flew off for a week's holiday in winter time to lie in the sun. Not to have been to Majorca was to court surprise. Team games were not dead, but less important. Only the star-studded football teams filled their grounds; cricketers to make money had to stimulate their supporters with one-day 'cliff-hangers'; women preferred mixed clubs and individual games to hockey and lacrosse, if they bothered about games at all. Men still wanted to show off special skills but played few team games if they were not particularly good at them. Swimming grew in popularity, so did squash rackets, and golf in England at last broke through the class barrier. There was much congregating of men and women in large numbers at Butlin's and other holiday camps, at swimming pools, in caravan parks and at rallies of various kinds.

At the heart of all this change was the motor car, no longer the status symbol of the middle classes but an accepted necessity of three-quarters of the nation's families. Many families had two cars, freeing stay-at-home wives for activities of their own, or allowing the millions of working wives to go to work in the same way as their husbands. To most men and many women the car was a pastime in itself; it symbolized freedom and fun. The entertainments industry was challenged; it had to think up new ways of catering for thousands who were less inhibited than earlier customers in their choice of what they wished to do. They were willing to travel, even out to dinner, but what they wanted at the end of the journey was 'life', something to counterbalance the boredom of their jobs.

Alan Sillitoe summed up this mood in *Saturday Night and Sunday Morning*:

> For it was Saturday night, the best and bingiest glad-time of the week, one of the fifty-two holidays in the slow-turning Big Wheel of the year, a violent preamble to a prostrate Sabbath. Piled up passions were exploded on Saturday night, and the effect of a week's monotonous graft in the factory was swilled out of your system in a burst of goodwill.

So, it was no longer 'get away from it all' in the sense of seeking peace and quiet, but get away and into an atmosphere of stimulation and excitement. And always with a crowd and always with music. In many ways it was wonderful to watch and admirable to experience this new-found camaraderie of man, but those still seeking holiday peace were driven, literally, to the hills.

The motor car also made a difference to play in everyday life. The wife was now a partner and a driver. On winter Saturdays the attraction of the football match was often not so strong as the need to get the shopping done (to many a Saturday entertainment in itself), the car fixed and everything ready for a Sunday trip to relations or friends. Restaurants appeared everywhere. Eating out was now a major enjoyment for thousands, and particularly for those whose children were already (at an earlier age than before) going their separate ways. Perhaps of all the changes to meet this new situation the most desirable was the re-creation of the public house. There were now good ones everywhere, some justly famed for their evening meals, others for the imagination shown in providing snacks at the bar. Long distances, comparatively, were travelled to reach them, not because there were not others closer by; simply for the change—at least before the petrol price increases of 1975.

By that date the only kind of mass enjoyment denied to more than half the population because of cost was messing about in boats. Here the richer remnant were still at an advantage and they found new allies as their ranks were swollen. Like the caravanners they congregated in their special harbours or moorings, rivalling one another in the size of their boats. They

Post-war picnics were home from home affairs, complete with music. Older picnickers brought tables

enjoyed themselves very much, partly because, like the motorists of the previous generation, they were pioneers.

One result of these changes was a new set of worries for directors of the big sporting arenas. Football was worst hit because, like cricket, it needed to attract large crowds on many days in the year. Besides the motor car it had, it thought, another natural enemy in television. Most live football matches were banned and showings of matches were regularly on Saturday evening and Sunday afternoons. Since the games shown were usually those between superior teams, or teams doing particularly well in lower leagues, the lukewarm follower was satisfied with these, and even the faithful had his faith undermined if his own team was showing no commensurate skill. Managers could fulminate about lack of support and argue that a football lover had a duty to shout encouragement to his club; in fact this view of loyalty, where play was concerned, had grown old fashioned and was reserved for the supporters of those players who gave them something to shout about. Play ceased to be play for the spectator if it included an element of compulsion and there was no fun.

Contributing to falling gates in the 1970s was the young spectator violence. Some said it was the fault of schools and parents; others blamed it on the lack of outlets for aggression and to a new generation finding the now tightly controlled play too unexciting for its taste. This view was upheld by those who watched the rival troops of young supporters take up their positions before a match, engaging one another immediately with taunts and chants. It seemed all too obvious that this was their play and the match only the vehicle which gave them opportunity for aggressive display. The Football Association was unimpressed; it continued its campaign to make the game less of a physical contact one and television screens inevitably included close-ups of wagging fingers and heated exchanges between players and referees. Football players, it seemed, must be gentlemen, while down the road the gentlemen of the Rugby scrum were still allowed a great deal of latitude which the smaller crowds most thoroughly enjoyed.

Cricket solved its own difficulties in an unexpected way. It became big business by introducing one-day matches with definite results (weather permitting, as curiously it mostly did). The purists and the lovers of the peace of cricket were shocked and there was certainly something in their argument that the rules of one-day cricket had changed the game. But mostly the crowds loved it, turned out in big numbers on Sundays, and made the match on many county grounds a family occasion. There were three competitions: the Gillette Cup, a knock-out competition between the counties on a limited over basis (started 1963), the John Player's (Sunday) county league (1969) and the Benson and Hedges league cup, starting in four area leagues (1972). Nothing like the scenes at the Gillette Cup final at Lord's on more than one occasion had previously been witnessed in English cricket. It was crowd participation at the highest level of enjoyment without rancour. It was not the same at test matches. The decorum of the old days had vanished and in its place had come, with the influx of West Indians and Indians into the population, a paler reflection of overseas boisterous behaviour at these contests between countries. Some of it was amusing and, since the bottle and

Successful 1st and 2nd division footballers still drew big crowds on a fine day

The teenage football followers were not always violent but railway officials usually feared the worst

can throwing in England up to 1975 was fairly mild, it seemed a harmless expenditure of emotion. But that was not to say that everyone enjoyed it.

Other spectator sports did not suffer comparable upheavals. Horse racing had its troubles but by and large the same races held the general public's attention while the addicts continued to study form. Motor racing now had a big following, the dogs were still popular and, when the personalities were right, athletics attracted many people. The biggest change was in golf. Before World War II spectators were few; now large crowds for the major tournaments scampered after their heroes all day, holding their breath one minute before streaking off to get a good view of the next shot. Golf crowds were unique; they were composed of current players. Few players of any game can have played their strokes in front of so many who knew, from weekly experience, just how difficult the stroke might be.

All major games, with the exception perhaps of football, had been helped enormously by the coverage of television. Racing, football of all three kinds, motor racing, cricket, golf, swimming, athletics, tennis, winter sports, boxing and wrestling were regularly on view, with one addition of a sport, show jumping, that many liked to imagine themselves performing without much hope of doing so. Some popular recreations, squash rackets and boating, were unlucky; either they provided too little scope for the cameras or progress was too monotonous or slow. For a long time opinions differed about the effect of television on the games themselves. Some thought that all games would become like a theatre, a matter for professionals, with too few

Motor racing celebrities Moss, Schell, Fangio and Hawthorn drew the crowds in the 1950s

A day no athlete wishes to forget, Roger Bannister running the four-minute mile, 1954

playing themselves at less exalted levels. Others thought the opposite, that the standards shown acted as a spur and encouragement to those who had the skills. What was certain was that television was doing for sport what radio had done for music, creating a vast new audience whose enjoyment was markedly increased by new-found expertise.

Television also fitted in well with the increase in international play. Costly though it was, air travel had become a commonplace for teams of all kinds but particularly for those playing football on the European continent. Because all could now share in the excitement, there were new competitions: the European Championship, the European Championship for under-23s, the European Cup-Winners' Cup, the European Fairs Cup and others. All meant much travelling mid-week for competing teams but financially it was worth it, as the fees paid to top footballers and for transfers proved. Television also kept an eye on athletes all over the world; it introduced thousands, who had never before seen them, to the pleasures and perils of skiing and sleigh rides, it made heroes and heroines of ice-skaters and swimmers and generally took every possible opportunity to cover big events because it knew its audience would be there. The culmination of effort, every four years, was at the Olympic Games, a fortnight's feast that was, some felt, too rich to be digestible.

However, as the standards of national and international performances in individual sports rose, so in team games at schools and colleges they continued to fall. It was no longer necessary at school to be good at games in order to achieve social recognition. A boy or girl was permitted to make a choice. He or she had every opportunity, even old-fashioned encouragement, to play games, but if hobbies were preferred, they could be indulged. Once again it was music that was the chief beneficiary. Thousands of children all over the country were learning instruments, many of them playing well enough to join, first, youth orchestras and then orchestras in the town. 'Pop' was receiving even greater support and from being a trivial recreation was transformed into an international society of zealots with an international knowledge of bands, music and rhythmic dance. This was another side of international life unknown to their parents. All youth seemed ready to travel on the slenderest means to join in festivals all over Europe and perhaps beyond. Classical music was not neglected, and it was no longer a case, as it had been in the thirties, of either/or. Many of those who queued for hours to attend a Promenade Concert at the often over-crowded Albert Hall were to be found next evening at a pop or folk event. For older people the acceptance of modern pop was far from easy. For them, mostly, it continued to be noise; for the young it began at the disco and seemed likely to continue throughout life.

Finding the peace which eludes them for the rest of the week, fishermen on the Thames

Potholing has a strong fascination for a dauntless band of younger men and women

The theatre showed no equal development. In spite of drama festivals there was no general rise in the standard of amateur acting and the professional stage remained the enjoyment of the few. The plays were quite different from those of the thirties. Nothing for a long period was sweet or sentimental. There were few drawing rooms, no butlers or smart amusing maids—except in farce—and if there was a bed it was probably in an attic or in sordid (realistic?) surroundings. Plays were obsessed with problems of self-understanding and the unspiritual aspects of the realities of life: they were played in commonplace sitting rooms, bed-sits and kitchens, all places where, the dramatists said, the *real* conversations took place. Influenced by Brecht and the Capeks of earlier decades but by British dramatists hardly at all, there was interesting work by John Osborne (*Look Back in Anger*), Arnold Wesker and Harold Pinter, but it had only a narrow appeal and compared not at all with the reception on television of such interpretations of modern life as *Till Death Us Do Part* or *Steptoe and Son*.

There were stage successes, of course, although very modest in terms of numbers. Some of these, with historical relevance, were made into even more successful films. *A Man for All Seasons* was one of them. By and large, however, the stage failed to move into the age of the common man, and added little to his play, which in this genre was satisfied by television, more aware of his needs and with constant opportunity to vary the scene. In the face of this competition the second-rate film practically disappeared. For a time cinemas were closing all over the country but, once the pruning was over, the few remaining blossomed with strong pictures to suit varying tastes. The censors were busy because of films of sex and violence, but a really good film usually won support whatever its type. Westerns could still fill the house, so could historical drama, and the reign of Walt Disney's fantasy was prolonged.

The film show in the sixties did more than the football match to satisfy the youth bulge (of population statistics) with scenes of violence. There was also a lust for sexual display, an aspect of violence which, with the new freedom, some producers did their 'best' to meet, as did some publishers. At its 'worst', the so-called literature was imported; at its more moderate it was helped along by reputable publishing firms with their stimulatingly covered paperbacks or jackets. The public remained its own judge, the unexpurgated edition of *Lady Chatterley's Lover* establishing a new standard of propriety. Curiously enough, the old tradition from Chaucer to Edwardian music hall also persisted. Middle-class wives, who would have hesitated at the works of Edna O'Brien, cheerfully bought *Rugby Songs* for the Christmas stockings of their Rugger playing husbands as if in acknowledgment of a morality that accepted eternally that boys would be boys.

After a lean period smaller bookshops began to flourish again. They could not rely on the London West End bestseller list or the books reviewed in the Sunday newspapers. Yet they sold more poetry, more Penguin classics and Pelican non-fiction than most older people found believable, for they sold it to the young. Fantasy was also in. It did not stop at science fiction, popular though this was, but had remarkable sales of *The Lord of the Rings*, *The Hobbit* and *Watership Down*. It was a paperback revolution, but one that

*'Away from it all' is the ambition of many
walkers on the coasts and hills*

*Not everyone wishes to be alone on holiday.
Blackpool is a satisfactory spot for these*

justified the belief that something had been done in schools to stimulate imagination. The same was true of record shops. With money in the pocket, and no incentive to save, hundreds of thousands of pounds were spent weekly on records, record-playing equipment, transistor sets and tape-recorders and tapes. Music was very big business and the interest of the young in it suggested that here was a permanent change.

For the leisure industry there was need for constant adjustment as soon as it was realized that the main market was greater and markedly different from the middle class demands of the twenties and thirties. Until 1974, when doubts arose, it was taken almost for granted that shorter hours of work and higher wages were the future's prospects, and that the filling of leisure hours profitably to all was a major concern. It was to be real play, a matter of individual choice, not directed by the industry but meeting demand.

This vision was shared by the local authorities. Already they were supplying more recreation centres, swimming baths, adventure playgrounds and a dozen other ways of filling up the leisure hours, including Sundays. Of the several committees involved, that of education was as busy as any with adult courses. It aimed to supply courses on anything that was declared worthwhile and likely to broaden and deepen individual enjoyment of life. The results were uneven but thousands benefited, finding unpremeditated pleasure in perhaps archaeology, pottery or painting. They also learnt languages, practised flower arranging, improved their cooking or dressmaking, made soft toys or jewellery, joined yoga and keep-fit classes, and generally searched the prospectuses each year for fresh suggestions. Guitar playing and 'do it yourself' were high on the list of new accomplishments, matching the sales of paperbacks on most adult education subjects in the bookshops.

Part of this play was social: the pleasure of working together in a group. Fifteen to twenty amateur gardeners united in a class soon found, under an amiable tutor, that they looked forward to the fellowship created by a shared interest as much as they appreciated the knowledge acquired. Gardening was also an example of the use made of increased leisure. Less tied to vegetable production (before 1975), than in the past, there was more specialization and greater interest in propagation under glass. Festivals, particularly in village churches, brought together the grower and arranger of flowers. Group activity for the younger generation included demonstrating for or against issues of the moment, and taking part in sponsored feats to raise money for charity. The old found much to deplore in the play attitudes of the young but there was also much to admire. Many of these older critics were themselves regularly in the bingo halls.

Interest in open-air pursuits also increased, none more keenly than that off-shoot of ornithology, bird watching. The days of shooting birds, except by keepers and sportsmen, were over and men and women of all ages spent long periods waiting, with cameras sometimes, with binoculars always, for birds to appear on feeding grounds or on migration. Their play, like that of golfers, dominated their talk. Walking, too, was greatly encouraged by the opening of the Pennine Way and other paths and the development of National Parks. The less mobile could now visit by car the hundreds of big

(above) Mums and grandmas mostly have their regular flutters at the bingo halls

(below) Darts is a most popular pub game. Many pubs have teams and play in Leagues

houses and gardens open to the public. Climbing gained more adherents; so did pot-holing on a minor scale; only cycling suffered, injured by the motor age which threatened death or injury to the unwary and frightening parents into banning children's expeditions for fear of hurt.

There was still gambling, and because it was no longer a sin in the eyes of society, on an even wider scale. Betting shops were everywhere well patronized, sums spent on football pools were enormous and housewives fluttered in the bingo halls. There was an increase in the number of topical events on which the public considered placing a bet. Few came to grief, betting being for the majority well within their means and the vicious aspects known in some earlier periods were happily absent. There was a compulsion, but seemingly not great.

It was said at the beginning of this book that play was only true if it were performed with free will, for fun, and only for as long as the participant wanted it to go on. Nearly all the play at this time was of this kind. It was true that in the family grouping it was not possible for all its members to be playing at the same time; one or two of the group were likely to be acting under compulsion, or taking part in the interests of others, or making a compromise. Nevertheless, in young adult life, it was now accepted that the individual had the right to choose; there was no question of 'ought' or

Gambling is not confined to the pools and betting shops. This scene is at a Playboy Club

On a fine day a river trip can bring contentment as the world slips by

'should'. There was a loss to society and also to individuals in the difficulty of raising teams. 'Doing one's own thing' might well include playing in a team at a particular level, and this might be hard to find. Yet the phrase summed up play, now being achieved in multitudinous ways.

The complement to doing one's own thing was watching others do theirs. Television raised the standard of what was considered worth watching but the amount of spectator play enjoyed went far beyond conventional football, tennis, cricket and golf and spread into such activities as archaeology, travel and natural history. Everyone was aware that 'the box' brought the world into the living room and encouraged the wish to travel and the desire to try a hand at something different.

There remained the question of catharsis, defined in the dictionary as the purification of the emotions by vicarious experience. Nothing devised in this period took the place of Greek drama and the Roman amphitheatre, yet the emotions remained as strong as ever. The cinema helped a little although it often failed to purify, and left to himself the individual chose sometimes dangerously and wildly. As for those who wished to display skill or satisfy pride in physical perfection, he or she was never better suited. They could watch in person or on the television the diver leaving the high dive, the rider jumping in co-ordinated movement with his horse or the ski-jumper soaring into the air, and could associate themselves with any one of these and many more. Whether it was enough depended on the individual but at least seeing it assisted the mind's play.

By 1975 it could well be said that the world in the west had reached the point when all could play and all could enjoy, in exchange for a moderate amount of work, something like the life experienced for centuries only by the rich. But by 1975 the seed of doubt was sown. What had appeared a few years back to be inevitable advance to even better and easier times seemed now in jeopardy. Would it all last? Could any society survive when all took so much interest in play? Had too much money, thought and time been spent on play? Was 1975 the end of one period and the beginning of the next?

☆ *ACKNOWLEDGEMENTS* ☆

The author and publishers wish to thank the following for their kind permission to reproduce photographs and illustrations in this book: Barnaby's Picture Library for photographs on pages 33, 35 (above), 59, 137 (all pictures), 143, 145 (both pictures), 147, 148 (both pictures), 151, 153, 155, 156, 159, 163 (both pictures), 164, 165, 166 (below), 168 (both pictures), 174, 175; Bodleian Library, pages 22 (below), 29, 64; British Library, pages 13, 21, 22 (above), 23, 27, 35 (below), 37, 42, 43 (both pictures), 45, 47, 49, 51 (both pictures), 63, 89, 116; British Library, pages 13, 21, 22 (above), 23, 27, 35 (below), 37, 42, 43 (both pictures), 45, 47, 49, 51 (both pictures), 63, 89, 116; British Library, photos by Freeman, 87 (both pictures), 92, 95 (all pictures), 97, 101 (below), 106, 109, 110, 113 (below), 135; Camera Press, pages 15 (below), 168 (above), 177, 179 (both pictures), 181 (above), 182, 183; Simon Wingfield Digby, page 57 (below); Fotomas Index, page 119 (above); other photos by Freeman, pages 2, 13 (centre and below), 15 (above and centre), 41 (all pictures), 53, 65, 66, 74, 79, 81, 83 (both pictures), 85 (above and below), 86, 90, 99, 101 (both pictures), 110 (both pictures), 113 (above), 120, 121, 130 (below), 132, 140; William J. Howes, page 176; Viscount de l'Isle, page 57 (above); MCC, page 131; National Gallery, page 69; National Portrait Gallery, page 77; Radio Times Hulton Picture Library, pages 133, 152, 157, 158, 161, 166 (above), 181 (below); Tate Gallery, page 98; Reginald Thompson, page 91; Traube Photography, pages 173 (both pictures), 184; Victoria and Albert Museum, page 85 (centre).

While every endeavour has been made to trace copyright owners of photographs used in this book, the publishers apologise for any oversight which might have occurred.